YOUR TAILOR-MADE TRIP STARTS HERE

Tailor-made trips and unique adventures crafted by local experts

Rough Guides has been inspiring travellers with lively and thought-provoking guidebooks for more than 35 years. Now we're linking you up with selected local experts to craft your dream trip. They will put together your perfect itinerary and book it at local rates.

Don't follow the crowd – find your own path.

HOW ROUGHGUIDES.COM/TRIPS WORKS

STEP 1

Pick your dream destination, tell us what you want and submit an enquiry.

STEP 2

Fill in a short form to tell your local expert about your dream trip and preferences.

STEP 3

Our local expert will craft your tailor-made itinerary. You'll be able to tweak and refine it until you're completely satisfied.

STEP 4

Book online with ease, pack your bags and enjoy the trip! Our local expert will be on hand 24/7 while you're on the road.

POCKET **ROUGH GUIDE**

BELFAST

WEEKENDER

Trip tips

10 Things not to miss

From imposing architecture, a Victorian legacy and a proud industrial heritage, to a diverse, spectacular landscape, here at a glance are just a few of the attractions Belfast and Northern Ireland have to offer.

∧ **Botanic Gardens.** Popular since Victorian times, this colourful park features a Tropical Ravine and 1839 Palm House. See page 53.

∧ **Crown Liquor Saloon.** A Victorian bar that is so ornate the National Trust bought it. See page 22.

∧ **Causeway Coastal Route.** Hit the road alongside Co. Antrim's spectacular coast, past traditional fishing villages and stunning views. See page 90.

> **Giant's Causeway.** A UNESCO World Heritage Site comprised of hexagonal basalt columns, formed, allegedly, by mythical giant Finn McCool. See page 92.

∧ **City Hall.** This impressive copper-domed architectural jewel dominates the city centre. See page 28.

∧ **Grand Opera House.** This striking Victorian theatre hosts everything from drama to ballet and musicals. See page 24.

∧ **Ulster Folk Museum.** Restored buildings bring local history and tradition to life. See page 109.

∨ **Titanic heritage.** The doomed liner was built here in the early twentieth century; Titanic Belfast commemorates the legacy. See page 84.

∨ **Londonderry/Derry.** Multi-monikered walled city, besieged in 1689, now famous for its lively social and cultural scene. See page 94.

∨ **Parliament Buildings.** Opened in 1932, Stormont is the setting for Northern Ireland's devolved government. See page 87.

Belfast Castle.

INTRODUCTION TO
Belfast

Belfast and Northern Ireland have emerged triumphant from the Troubles, rebuilding communities and promoting their urban vitality and spectacular landscapes.

Without its baggage of troubles, and the resulting three decades of media coverage that sent its flames around the globe, Belfast could have been seen in another light: as an extravagance of pubs and churches; as a seaport rich in Victorian architecture, where the ill-fated *Titanic* was built; as a hub for the manufacture of Irish linen; as host to a fine university; as home to the late George Best, a footballing legend.

But Belfast was abandoned to a different fate and a troubled period of history. There was scant mention in those years of the in-your-face humour, of pubs pulsing with music, and of pints downed in the *Crown Liquor Saloon*.

Since the late 1990s, Belfast has realised its pre-Troubles potential. The *crack* (see page 38) is now enjoyed in hip bars and hotels as well as traditional pubs. You can catch a cutting-edge DJ in a city-centre club and eat remarkably well before setting off on excursions to some of the finest

scenery in the British Isles. More than a century after its golden age, Belfast has finally come into its own.

Position and landscape

Belfast is cradled among a saucer of hills in the northeast of the island of Ireland, hooking around the head of a broad sea lough at the mouth of the River Lagan, which flows into the Irish Sea. It is the capital of the six counties of Northern Ireland (Antrim, Armagh, Londonderry, Down, Fermanagh and Tyrone), founded in 1921, and is part of the United Kingdom (UK).

Northern Ireland occupies just seventeen percent of the island's landmass but contains a high proportion of its physical attractions. The North Antrim Coast Road is a marvel of engineering. Behind it unfurls the nine Glens of Antrim, a world of rugged scenery and weather-beaten farmers. On the northern coast, past long stretches of sandy beach, lies the Giant's Causeway, a remarkable geological curiosity. County Fermanagh's lakelands and Lough Neagh, the largest sheet of inland water in the British Isles, are a draw for anglers and boating enthusiasts. Spectacular mountain ranges – the Sperrins and the Mournes – complete the picture.

The Ulster character

Instead of the soft, beguiling Irish brogue, the Northern Irish accent is harder, less melodious. If the Southern accent has the rhythm of a lullaby, then Belfast's has the cadence of

Mother Daughter Sister sculpture by artist Ross Wilson.

Bittles Bar.

punk. Some say it is an accent that adapts particularly well to rabble-rousing oratory, as exemplified by the province's best-known former governmental First Minister, the late Reverend Ian Paisley.

There's a twist to a well-known saying that sums up the sometimes dour, somewhat pessimistic, but always pragmatic, Northern Irish attitude: 'Every silver lining has a cloud'. The people are endearingly, refreshingly and sometimes alarmingly down to earth. Straight-talk and self-deprecation are considered important, even essential, traits.

The 'joke with a jag' may be barbed, but it's as often as not pointed inwards. Yet the warmth of the welcome and people's willingness to engage is undeniably seen in abundance too.

Turbulence to peace

As a result of the Irish War of Independence, 1919–21, six of the nine counties of the province of Ulster became known as Northern Ireland, remaining part of the UK (with self-governance). The British government,

glad to be rid of the troublesome Irish Question, ignored the problems in their forgotten province. But by the 1960s civil unrest was prevalent with students swelling the ranks of the Civil Rights Movement, marching to demand an end to discrimination in social housing and employment for Catholics. As old animosities flared up, rioting took place in August 1969, a moribund IRA resurrected itself and militant Protestant groups formed, leading to the deployment of British soldiers on the streets.

It took thirty years, the abolition of self-governance, the imposition of direct rule from Westminster, the creation of a Dublin–London political axis, major population shifts and the loss of more than 3200 lives before the province voted in 1998 for peace through a power-sharing Assembly. But mutual suspicions remained, and political deadlock forced the British government to suspend the Assembly until trust could be established.

It was touch and go, but five years of direct rule from London ended on 8 May 2007 when Ian Paisley and Sinn Féin's Martin McGuinness,

Police charge a crowd of rioting demonstrators in 1870.

Go green and explore

It's not just the scenery that's green in Northern Ireland. Belfast scored serious eco-credentials when it was ranked eleventh out of 100 destinations in the 2023 Global Destination Sustainability Index. Along with the Belfast Resilience Strategy – the city's first climate plan, launched in 2020 – plans are underway to build a zero-emissions, climate-resilient economy within a generation. The city's network of walking and cycling paths has mushroomed over the past decade; a highlight is the Lagan Towpath, with around 1.5 million people taking to the 11-mile riverside trail every year. For information on walks in Belfast and Northern Ireland, visit www.walkni.com.

who had never talked to each other before, sat down together as Northern Ireland's new leaders.

Northern Ireland's political landscape was further complicated by the UK voting to leave the European Union in 2016, with Unionists fearful of an economic border between Northern Ireland and the rest of the UK. The Democratic Unionist Party (DUP) withdrew from the devolved Assembly in 2022, once more throwing into question the future of Stormont's power-sharing government. The two main parties in Northern Ireland are currently Sinn Féin and the DUP.

A new Belfast

Neither planners nor bombers were kind to Belfast. In the 1960s, a lacklustre provincial civil service failed to recognise the vernacular environment that architect Charles Lanyon had created a century before.

Great buildings were demolished, replaced by flaking concrete. The bombers had a go at much that was left, leaving a city rich in unplanned parking lots, with a smattering of fine buildings standing out. The decline of the shipbuilding industry left the banks of the Lagan lying idle and looking derelict.

At the first signs of peace, flyovers swept through inner-city villages, and Belfast rekindled its affection for its potent Victorian and Edwardian heritage. Laganside Corporation was a public body formed in 1989 to regenerate the Laganside area. It captured a public imagination fired by Victor Robinson's keynote Waterfront Hall, and drew up plans for the historic Cathedral Quarter, now home to trendy bars, tourist-friendly pubs and upmarket restaurants.

From City Hall south to the university, an ever-growing crop of bars and nightclubs sprang up across the streets, attracting revellers from Britain and further afield. Growth has snowballed with the development of the docks area and the opening of both the Metropolitan Arts Centre (The MAC) and the boat-shaped Titanic Belfast visitor attraction, boosting tourism to the area.

Taking it easy in the Botanic Gardens.

Food and drink

The past couple of decades have seen both expansion and experimentation in the foodie scene in Belfast, and throughout the province. Vegetarians and vegans won't have a problem finding meat-free dishes – if not entire eateries – now dedicated to them. Look out, too, for the provenance of local produce on menus, right down to the names of the farms the potatoes and meat came from, and the harbour where that day's catch landed. Farmers' markets are where you'll find small-scale producers offering everything from hand-produced cheeses and chutneys to locally grown mushrooms and microgreens. With dining options ranging from budget-friendly fish-and-chip shops and pub grub, to decadent afternoon teas in ornate hotels and inventive dishes by celebrity chefs, there's no shortage of options.

Northern Irish cooking

Two distinctive styles of cooking have started to emerge in recent years. One looks to home and tradition, with chefs such as Paula McIntyre exploring their Ulster-Scots culinary heritage. The other emphasises fusion and flourish, serving up a lighter, more modern twist, and incorporating global ingredients.

Whiskey from Titanic Distillers.

But traditional dishes, usually comprising some combination of potatoes, meat and bread, will always have a place in the hearts of Northern Irish people. No visit would be complete without experiencing an Ulster Fry, different to the fry-ups of the rest of the UK and Ireland by its use of soda bread and potato farls – fried until crisp and golden. Bacon, sausages, an egg, a tomato and maybe some mushrooms complete the picture – and, of course, all washed down with a pot of tea.

Local specialities

Champ: mashed potatoes with lots of butter, warm milk and chopped scallions (spring or green onions).
Dulse: a dried, salty, seaweed snack, historically harvested by fishermen to supplement their income when fishing was slack.
Potato bread farl: a dense, earthy flatbread, made with potatoes, flour, butter and salt.
Soda bread farl: thick, chunky soft bread, first baked in nineteenth-century Ireland when local peasants added buttermilk and baking soda to help the dough rise.

Follow the culinary trail on a Belfast Food Tour.

Wheaten bread: a moist brown bread made with whole-wheat flour.

Yellow man: crunchy golden confectionery that resembles honeycomb.

Fifteens: a much-loved sweet tray bake, made with digestive biscuits, glacé cherries, marshmallows, condensed milk and desiccated coconut.

Farm to fork

A mild climate and green and fertile land make for excellent agricultural conditions. Specialist farmers and artisan makers are plentiful in Northern Ireland and the region is rapidly gaining a reputation for its superb local producers: Lough Neagh is Europe's greatest source of eels; Finnebrogue venison has put Northern Ireland on the culinary map in top restaurants; the much sought-after Comber potato is grown in the arable farmland of County Down. Kettyle of Fermanagh produces extra-mature, dry-aged beef from its grass-fed native herd; and Castlescreen Farm is a popular choice when it comes to grass-fed Dexter beef, lamb, free-range pork and pastured chicken.

Market fresh

Soak up the atmosphere at Ireland's oldest covered market, St George's in Belfast, built in 1896 (www.belfast

A lively atmosphere at St George's Market.

Bushmills Whiskey

Bushmills Irish Whiskey is the original and best-known whiskey to come out of the Old Bushmills Distillery in County Antrim. This smooth, rich blend of single malt and single grain has been produced for four centuries, since King James I granted a licence to distil in 1608. The whiskey is processed the same way today as it was four hundred years ago – aged a minimum of five years in oak casks specially selected to bring out the golden hue, using only 100 percent barley.

city.gov.uk/stgeorgesmarket), which is abundant with fresh fish and seafood, creamy Irish cheeses, meats, breads and cakes, as well as live music. Farmers' markets are great if you are on a self-catering holiday, planning a picnic or just wanting to try authentic local foods. The pick of the bunch are Inns Cross Market (www.visitlisburncastlereagh. com); Saintfield Saturday Market (www.discoversaintfield.com); Tyrone Farmers' Market in Dungannon and Omagh (www.visitmidulster.com); the Comber Farmers' Market in County Down (www.combermarket.co.uk), and the Causeway Speciality Market in Coleraine (www.causewaycoast andglens.gov.uk).

Eating out price guide

Each restaurant and café reviewed in this Guide is accompanied by a price category, based on the cost of a two-course meal (or similar) for one, including a non-alcoholic drink.

£££ = over £35

££ = £20–35

£ = under £20

Late-night shopping in Donegall Square.

TOUR 1

Around the city centre

This 2-mile (4km) walk, in half a day, takes in some of Belfast's prime attractions and venerable institutions, making it the perfect introduction to this vibrant city.

The city centre of Belfast saw its fair share of turbulence during the Troubles but has emerged as an attractive area with a mix of grandiose architectural gems, modern shops and stylish restaurants.

Welcome Centre

An excellent starting point is the **Belfast Welcome Centre ❶** (9 Donegall Square North; www.visit belfast.com; free) where you can pick up informative brochures, buy souvenirs and gifts, and seek advice on accommodation, attractions, tours and transport from the multilingual staff. The centre also stocks a range of maps and general information on Northern Ireland, and you can purchase tickets for Translink buses and trains, as well

Highlights

- Linen Hall Library
- Scottish Provident Institution
- Ulster Hall
- Crown Liquor Saloon
- Grand Opera House
- Royal Belfast Academical Institution

as some tours and events. There's free wi-fi and left-luggage facilities (charges apply), if you want to explore the city unencumbered.

Linen Hall Library

Just a few doors along, at 17 Donegall Square North, **Linen Hall ❷** (www.linenhall.com; free) is the oldest library in Belfast, established in 1788,

Researching Narnia

Linen Hall Library has a fascinating selection of books by or about C.S. Lewis (1898–1963, see also Tour 9), the Belfast-born-and-raised Christian writer and author of the *Narnia Chronicles*. Visitors can access all the library's collections, though only members can borrow books. The children and young adults section also features books written in Irish and Ulster-Scots, as well as publications celebrating inclusivity and diversity.

and it has played a vigorous part in Belfast's cultural life. Thomas Russell, a founding member, was arrested at its earlier premises in Ann Street for his part in the United Irishmen uprising of 1798.

The present location is a three-storey, five-bay building with stucco mouldings on its windows. The most eminent of the architects of Victorian Belfast, the prolific Charles Lanyon (you'll see his name a lot in this book, so busy was he building Belfast), designed the building as a linen warehouse of greyish-yellowish brick with a dressing of Victorian detail on its Georgian proportions. Inside, an impressive brass-railed stone staircase leads to the muted calm of reading rooms, its walls lined with heavy wooden glass-fronted bookcases and stained-glass windows commemorating famous writers.

Sensitively restored in 2001, it now boasts a modern café with views over Donegall Square and a well-stocked shop of literary souvenirs. The library is still a venue for regular cultural events, including literary talks, drama, poetry readings and exhibitions, but its main attraction remains its unique collections. Chief among them is a

major body of Irish and Local Studies works, but many visitors come for its unrivalled Northern Ireland Political Collection, dating from the Troubles and now running to 350,000 items. For those interested in cartographic prison history, a map of H-Block 7 used in the IRA Maze escape in 1983, is displayed in a cabinet in the political research room.

Donegall Square West

Just opposite, facing the west side of City Hall, you can trace the industrial heritage of Belfast from carvings high up on the Glasgow blonde sandstone of the vast **Scottish Provident Institution ❸** on Donegall Square West. The building has almost as much Edwardian pomp and presence as the City Hall. Cherubs work at their ABCs on a Gutenberg printing press, and easily identified are an anchor and hammer for shipbuilding, plus skeins

The book-lined walls of the Linen Hall Library.

of linen yarn and a spinning wheel, the tools of ropemaking.

Below, less finely carved heads, copied from Thomas Fitzpatrick's work on what is now the *Malmaison* hotel (see page 125) in Victoria Street, represent the people to whom a commercially buoyant city exported its

An area once home to many of the world's great linen manufacturers.

goods: the etchings, to modern eyes, are stereotypical, verging on caricature: an Englishman, benign and plump; an Asian tribal chief; an African; and a Native American with high cheekbones.

Modern Belfast

With clear views of the City Hall, *Hell Cat Maggie's* (formerly *The Apartment*), sums up a lot about the new breed of Belfast bars. There's the quirky name for a start; the original Hell Cat Maggie was said to be an outlaw in 1840s Manhattan. Born in Ireland, she went on to raise hell in New York. As well as nods to the past, with its open brickwork, eclectic vintage bric-a-brac and live traditional music nights, it also offers modern craft beers, trendy cocktails and all-day dining. During the 1970s and 1980s, the Troubles meant that few people would have socialised in the city centre. That has all now changed.

Linen Quarter

South of the City Hall lies the Linen Quarter, once known as Linenopolis because, by the late nineteenth century, Belfast had the largest linen industry in the world. This brought wealth, employment and population growth as well as associated warehouses and grand buildings. Walk east along Donegall Square South to the former **Yorkshire House**, on the corner of Donegall Square South and Linenhall Street. This former 1860s warehouse is adorned with a series of 'heroes' heads' between the ground-floor windows, including George Washington, Isaac Newton, Homer and Michelangelo. It is now the luxury **Ten Square Hotel** ❹ (see page 125).

Turn right onto Linenhall Street to view some of the original sandstone buildings built during the linen trade era. Duck down Franklin Street and at the end head south onto Bedford Street, which is littered with former linen warehouses and home to the imposing, modern *Grand Central Hotel* at Nos. 9–15 (see page 19; www.grandcentralhotelbelfast.com).

Ulster Hall

Further along Bedford Street you will see the Italianate stucco of W.J. Barre's **Ulster Hall** ❺ (34 Bedford Street; www.ulsterhall.co.uk). Completed in 1862 as a ballroom, it was once the largest music hall in the British Isles. Its airy spaciousness and excellent acoustics also provided a resounding platform for the rallies of the Irish nationalist politicians Charles Stewart Parnell and Patrick Pearse, and for David Lloyd George, British prime minister from 1916 to 1922. Charles Dickens read from *A Christmas Carol* and *The Pickwick Papers* here in January 1869.

In 1980, pop fans dancing at a Dexys Midnight Runners concert

Star performers

The Ulster Hall stages all kinds of concerts, from regular Ulster Orchestra gigs to rock and pop stars, comedians, beer festivals and much else. Rock fans will know that the Rolling Stones played the Hall in 1964 and that Led Zeppelin's *Stairway to Heaven* had its stage debut here in 1971. The hall's mighty Mulholland Organ attracts a different fan base.

caused the floor to collapse (yet the concert kept going). In 2000, the Dalai Lama appeared as a guest of Amnesty International.

It is also the home of the highly regarded Ulster Orchestra and, despite its heritage, it is especially good at catering to twenty-first century needs, supporting accessibility, diversity and inclusion with, among other things, wheelchair access and an autism-friendly environment.

Beside the Ulster Hall, you'll find the elegantly decorated *Harlem Café* (www.harlemcafebelfast.com), a popular café to grab a bite and admire the antique-style decor.

Ulster Hall has played host to many famous figures.

The intricate fan-vaulted ceiling and striking stained-glass windows of St Malachy's Church.

St Malachy's Church

Turning left into Clarence Street, at the far end stands the dusky redbrick exterior of the Roman Catholic **St Malachy's Church** ❻ framed in the east. Designed by Thomas Jackson in 1880, this romantic church is a splendid turreted and castellated excursion into Tudor Gothic, its panelled door studded and topped with armorial shields. However, it is the church's interior that is the real treat for both the eyes and soul.

The dazzling fan-vaulted ceiling, a confection of creamy and frothy plasterwork, has been likened to a wedding cake turned inside out. In fact, it is an echo of Henry VII's Chapel in Westminster Abbey. Many of the original unpolished Irish oak fittings have disappeared but the organ is a century and a half old.

The church's chief benefactor, Captain Thomas Griffiths, understood that it would become the city's Roman Catholic cathedral, which accounts for the extravagance of decoration. The Great Bell installed in 1868 was once wrapped in felt to quieten its toll, for its resonance was claimed to interfere with distillation processes in Dunville's Whiskey Distillery, which once stood nearby. Along the southeast wall, gazing out in contemplative mood with his brown eyes and torn chocolate-hued coat, is the statue of the Ragged Saint, St Benedict Joseph Labre. The church offers live streaming services, so you can watch its Catholic mass from anywhere in the world.

Return west up Clarence Street, and catch a glimpse of the Black Mountain in the distance, before taking the second left and heading south along Linenhall Street to emerge onto Ormeau Avenue, where the city's reservoir once shimmered.

Ormeau Avenue

The **BBC Broadcasting House**, completed in 1838 and opened in 1941, is on the right of the avenue and is one of the finest Art Deco buildings in the city. Tours are available of the building, during which you might spot a local celeb or two going about their business. Almost unnoticed at the junction of Ormeau Avenue and Bedford Street, shaded beneath dusty trees, stands the **Thomas Thompson Memorial**, erected in memory of the founder of the city's Home for the Incurable. Many people walk by without a second glance. But look closely and you'll see that this red Aberdeen granite and sandstone former drinking fountain bears the legend: 'Who so drinketh of the water that I shall give him… shall never thirst again'. Thompson, a naval surgeon during the Napoleonic Wars, gained knowledge that enabled him to combat outbreaks of cholera, smallpox, dysentery and typhus in Belfast, not least during the Great Famine of the 1840s. Among the medieval-style heads carved beneath the spire is one of the good doctor himself, sporting luxuriant whiskers and a monocle.

Dublin Road

Follow **Dublin Road**, which runs south towards Shaftesbury Square. This is a fairly concentrated stretch of (largely Asian) restaurants, pubs, fast-food joints and coffee shops, beginning with the **Trademarket** (14–16 Dublin

A grand history

The 23-floor *Grand Central Hotel* cuts an imposing figure on Belfast's skyline, with a cocktail bar offering panoramic views across the city. But this is in fact Belfast's second *Grand Central*, its name linking old and new Belfast. The original *GC* (as it was known to locals), on Royal Avenue, opened in 1893. Its most celebrated room was Suite 217 which, over seventy-odd years, hosted many famous guests including Winston Churchill, Al Jolson, Bob Hope and cowboy film star, Gene Autry. In the 1960s it played host to The Rolling Stones and The Beatles. It closed in 1969 and was used as a barracks by the army until its subsequent demolition in the late 1980s, making way for CastleCourt Shopping Centre. The legend was reborn on Bedford Street in this 2018 version of the Victorian hotel of the same name.

Plans are underway to redevelop the BBC's Broadcasting House.

Ulster Hall stages concerts and festivals.

Road; www.trademarketbelfast.com) an outdoor street food market and retail hub, on the site of the former Movie House cinema.

When the restaurants started burgeoning in the 1990s, locals referred to the stretch as the Golden Mile, but the gold is no longer glistening as brightly as it used to. For authentic Chinese food at reasonable prices check out no-frills **The Chilli House** at No. 85. The Sichuan menu

Donegall Pass is a predominantly loyalist section between two republican areas.

features traditional favourites such as hotpot and *shui zhu* pork.

The Points (44 Dublin Road; www.pointsbelfast.com) serves up a wide selection of whiskey and ales, with traditional Irish music sessions a special feature. Looking a little out of place, further down the road, is the impressive Shaftesbury Square **Reformed Presbyterian Church**, which dates from 1890.

A detour left from Shaftesbury Square leads to a row of Asian supermarkets, restaurants and antique shops; Belfast's own mini Chinatown. This is Donegal Pass. The streets shooting off it are named after the trees in the wood it once passed through. Here, amid walls of loyalist graffiti, are some of Belfast's more interesting Chinese restaurants: **Same Happy**, at 40 Donegall Pass, and the compact Japanese haunt **Kamakura** (69 Donegall Pass; www.kamakurasushi.co.uk).

Shaftesbury Square
Return to **Shaftesbury Square**
❼, which itself is not particularly

Alternative Ulster

Founded by punk icon Terri Hooley, Good Vibrations was more than a record shop in late-1970s bomb-damaged Belfast – it was a way of life. The story of the shop, record label and Hooley's support of local punk bands – most famously The Undertones and Stiff Little Fingers – was turned into an eponymously named film in 2013. Today, a 2023 art mural at the shop's original site, at No.125 Great Victoria Street, commemorates the legacy of the Good Vibrations shops, music legend Hooley and the spirit of punk.

Grand Central Hotel.

prepossessing but it does shelter the architecturally dominating *FireStone* teppanyaki restaurant (www.thefirestone.co.uk) behind a gigantic glass frontage.

Named after the nineth earl of Shaftesbury, the public square was first recorded in 1887. Lord Shaftesbury was, among other titles bestowed on him, Lord Lieutenant of Belfast from 1904 to 1911, Lord Mayor of Belfast 1907 and Chancellor of Queen's University, Belfast from 1909 until 1923. Here, you can look up and see Belfast's modest answer to London's Piccadilly Circus neon advertisements, a large roadside digital billboard. The square was also known for its 1930s underground toilets, but, despite rumours over the years, they have yet to be repurposed as a bar or restaurant.

Great Victoria Street

Walking north, the route follows **Great Victoria Street**, once an avenue of fine redbrick and stucco terraced houses, now sadly neglected. The bombers of the 1970s continued what the planners had only in part achieved a decade earlier: the demotion of the street's

southern half to a mix of car parks and Brutalist 1960s constructions. Now little remains to tell of the street's glory days other than the stucco styling of the 1860s **Presbyterian Church** and the upper storeys of Victorian Richmond Terrace, north of the former Ulster Bank.

Further up the road is the entirely rebuilt **Hope International Christian Fellowship**, in a building that in the 1870s was the city's first synagogue. Vere Foster, the revolutionary educational philanthropist who helped many get to America in the famine years of the 1840s, lived and died at No. 115.

The atmospheric interior of the *Fitzwilliam Hotel.*

The polychrome brick building on the terrace's town side, **Shaftesbury Square Hospital**, designed by W.J. Barre in 1867, originally cared for those with ophthalmic problems and more recently for those suffering substance abuse. Water was a concern of the painter Paul Henry's father, minister at Great Victoria Street's original **Baptist Church** (now demolished and replaced with a modern building set back from the road on the same site) on the corner of Hope Street. He scandalised his 1870 congregation by announcing he had lost faith in total-immersion baptism. The street also houses **Ginger Bistro**, a lively restaurant for lunch or dinner serving local artisan beers.

On the other side of Hope Street, across Great Victoria Street, are the *Holiday Inn* and the *Hampton by Hilton* hotels, both huge modern buildings that ape the functional 1960s architecture that disfigured much of this area. They make up in value what their exteriors lack in aesthetic appeal.

Crown Liquor Saloon

Further on along Great Victoria Street is the Victorian Baroque **Crown Liquor Saloon** ❽ (www.nationaltrust.org.uk), Belfast's most famous pub. Bought in 1978 by the National Trust (on the recommendation of Sir John Betjeman who referred to it as a 'many-coloured cavern'), it was once the *Ulster Railway Hotel*, dating from 1895, the same year as the Opera House, and was also restored by Robert McKinstry.

It is a three-storey stucco building whose ground-floor bar is lavishly tiled in many colours and whose snugs – with bronze match strikers and a bell that wags a flag to summon service – are guarded by griffin and lions. The superb tiling, glasswork and ornamental woodwork are the creation of Italian craftspeople, brought to Belfast in the 1880s to

The richly burnished red and gold ceiling and decorative mosaic floor of the *Crown Liquor Saloon*, a fine example of Victoriana.

A whistle-stop ride around the city by bus.

and open-mouthed tourists. Despite moving into the social-media age, it remains one of the most authentic Victorian bars you could find.

Bars, buses and hotels

That is not something that can be said for **Robinsons Bars** (38–40 Great Victoria Street; www.robinsonsbar. co.uk), two doors north, which was bombed in 1991, gutting the interior, but then rebuilt with exteriors faithful to the original 1846 design. It is now home to five venues under one roof: the characterful *Saloon*; *Fibber Magees*, which hosts traditional Irish music sessions; the *Bistro* upstairs with iconic city views; and a traditional sports bar, the *Pool Loft*, up in the rafters.

Across the road fronting the entrance to the Europa Bus Centre, pose Louise Walsh's two life-sized bronzes (1992), titled *Monument to the Unknown Worker*. Amelia Street was once the bordello area, but the sculptor rejected the original idea of depicting sex workers, and instead made this in tribute to low-paid working women.

Here, too is the **Europa Hotel** (see page 124), from the comforts of which three decades of reporters covered the Troubles. It is notorious for being Europe's 'most bombed hotel', struck by 33 IRA bombs during

work on Catholic churches. Settle into a snug (booth) and order a plate of its signature fresh oysters, served on crushed ice.

The ceiling is embossed, the Guinness admirable, the waiters amenable and the customers a mixed bunch of stagehands, actors, journalists, travel writers, students

Taxi tours

One of the best ways to see Belfast is by registered taxi tour. These can be picked up in the city centre and take in the major and some lesser-known sights with the expert guides imparting their first-hand knowledge. Most tours of the city last around one hour and thirty minutes and you should come away knowing a great deal more about Belfast's troubled past and hopes for the future. Details from the Belfast Welcome Centre.

Murals on a taxi tour.

The Grand Opera House.

this tumultuous period. The *Europa* remains a part of Belfast nightlife.

Grand Opera House

The street's honeypot is another riot of Victorian Baroque, the **Grand Opera House** ❾ (www.goh.co.uk), although now somewhat dwarfed by the *Europa Hotel*. Designed by Frank Matcham and located on the corner of Glengall Street, the theatre hosts touring Shakespearean productions

and a Christmas pantomime, as well as West End musicals, opera, ballet performances and concerts.

High on its frontage, a naked bronze Mercury takes flight and Shakespeare looks on approvingly. But it is the interior that really delights, a riot of crimson and gold leaf with gilded elephant heads supporting the boxes and a heavenly ceiling mural. The theatre languished unloved as a cinema for much of the 1960s and was almost abandoned in the 1970s as a result of damage caused by a series of IRA terrorist bombs.

There's also a bright, spacious foyer, restaurant and bars and an intimate performance space, the Baby Grand. If you can't make it to a show, then the next best thing is to join a one-hour behind-the-scenes tour to follow in the footsteps of stars such as Charlie Chaplin and walk onto the iconic stage. Check with the theatre for current tour times.

Presbyterian Assembly Rooms

Diagonally opposite the Opera House, on the corner of Howard Street, is the rusticated sandstone Tudor Gothic bulk of the **Presbyterian Assembly Rooms** ❿ (www.presbyterianireland.

The Oriental-style architecture of the Grand Opera House.

Opera House greats

The Grand Opera House has played host to an impressive roster of international stars over the years. Sarah Bernhardt, Orson Welles and Laurel and Hardy have all graced the stage in their heyday. Italian tenor Luciano Pavarotti made his UK debut here in 1963 in Puccini's *Madame Butterfly*, and much-loved local boy Van Morrison's album, *Live at the Grand Opera House*, was recorded here in 1984.

The facade of the Royal Belfast Academical Institution (RBAI).

org), the essential Englishness of its mullioned windows made dour by Scots corbelling and a crown spire copied from St Giles' Cathedral, Edinburgh. The grand doorway arch and oriel window above are carved with biblical burning bushes and fourteen angels. The contest for its design in 1899 was clouded in unbiblical scandal, however – the winner being the church's architect who devised the competition. The exterior turret clock was the first in the British Isles to use electricity to drive its cogs and ring its twelve-bell carillon of twenty-eight tunes.

Today, the ground floor is given over to a conference room, exhibition space and multiple meeting rooms. The majestically polygonal Assembly Room upstairs, still one of the most impressive venues in Belfast, can also be hired for conferences as well as gigs and concerts.

Royal Belfast Academical Institution

North of Jury's Inn opposite the Assembly Rooms, Great Victoria Street becomes College Square East. It takes its name from the fine square lawn that complemented the Georgian symmetry of the dusky redbrick **Royal Belfast Academical Institution**. Now laid back beyond lawns, its spare elegance owing much to designs by the great English architect Sir John Soane, it is the city's finest building. Belfast's first major centre of learning, the RBAI was set up to cater for all the major denominations of Christianity and remains one of Northern Ireland's best boys' schools.

In 1902, debts forced the governors to sell off land. Amid controversy, the Municipal Technical Institute was built. The style is grand Baroque Revivalist, its four copper-domed turrets are impressive, and the city's coat of arms is set resolutely above the main doorway. This is now known as Belfast Metropolitan College – which also boasts a striking campus in the Titanic quarter.

But the loss of green sward in 1906 to build this temple to learning for the newly emerging industrial class destroyed the square's cachet as the

The statue on his plinth is of Dr Cooke, a Presbyterian cleric who was strongly against political liberalism.

address for surgeons and academics. The tall houses soon fell, first to commerce, then to the bomb.

Wellington Place

To return to the Linen Hall Library, cross the road and walk via Wellington Place, passing the 'Black Man' on his plinth. This 1876 statue of nineteenth-century, rabble-rousing Presbyterian cleric, Dr Henry Cooke, who opposed political liberalism, is not actually black but green. It is made of copper,

which has turned green after being oxidised by the elements.

The original figure, made of bronze, painted black and later moved to the City Hall, was of the 1885 Earl of Belfast. The reverend, whom Daniel O'Connell called 'Bully Cooke', has his back turned to the Academy whose notions on equality and religious tolerance he desperately opposed.

Very few of the original 1830s houses in **Wellington Place** remain. Named after the Duke of Wellington,

Novel Nouveau

The Art Nouveau shopfront of *The Lantern* restaurant at 58 Wellington Place is one of only a handful of buildings in Belfast to feature this style of design. The Georgian building's ornate entrance was adorned with colourful mosaics and intricate musical instruments around 1905 – a nod to its former role as Crymble's Music Shop.

Visit Belfast Welcome Centre.

who spent much of his boyhood at Annadale in the south of the city, the newest feature here is the family-friendly *Room2* – a self-proclaimed 'hometel' offering short- to long-term stays – on the corner with Queen Street. A few more steps along and we have returned to our starting place.

Eating out

Coco
7–11 Linenhall Street; www.cocobelfast.com.
The kitsch artwork, bold eclectic decor and glitter ball won't be to everyone's taste, but the food should be, with a good selection of meat, fish and vegetarian choices and a well-priced pre-theatre menu. £££

EDŌ
Capital House, 2 Upper Queen Street; www.edorestaurant.co.uk.
This buzzy tapas restaurant brings a slice of Spain to Belfast. Order a bunch of small plates to share and watch as the chefs rustle together the sizzling recipes in the open kitchen. The menu heaves with meats and seafood but vegans are catered for with a handful of plant-based dishes. £££

Ginger Bistro
7–8 Hope Street, just off Great Victoria Street; www.gingerbistro.com.
Locally sourced seafood is served with a culinary twist in dishes such as gin-cured salmon, while the meats come highly recommended at this always-busy, award-winning restaurant. The ingredient list prioritises local suppliers and there's a good selection of wines by the glass. £££

Hell Cat Maggie's
2 Donegall Square; www.hellcat-maggies.com.
With its shabby-chic interior, live music and extensive cocktail list, *Hell Cat Maggie's* has a buzzing atmosphere. The New York/Irish-inspired menu offers a range of hearty plates at reasonable prices, all served with a view of the City Hall. ££

Home
22 Wellington Place; www.homebelfast.co.uk.
Known for its fresh, seasonal food, with sustainability at its heart. Ingredients are sourced from local producers and transformed into creative, tasty dishes, with plenty of vegan, vegetarian and gluten-free options. Great cocktails too. ££

James St
19–21 James Street South; www.jamesst.co.uk.
One of Belfast's best restaurants since it opened in 2003. Executive head chef Ryan Stringer oversees an innovative menu that regularly picks up plaudits. The charcoal grill continues to take centre stage not just for the Tyrone steak and sustainable fish, but also for the duck and fresh vegetables. Elegant and classy, with top-notch service. £££

Linen Hall Cafe
17 Donegall Square North; www.linenhallcafe.com.
This family-run café is on the first floor of the Linen Hall Library. The all-day menu offers local favourites, such as Irish porridge, a breakfast fry and hearty stews. £

TRAIT
14 College Square East; www.traitcoffee.co.uk.
This colourful café has a warm community feel, a decent sustainability ethos, excellent coffee and tasty cakes and buns, made fresh in *TRAIT*'s own craft-bakery in Comber (where there is another branch of the café). £

A statue of Queen Victoria stands in the grounds of City Hall.

TOUR 2
City Hall to Donegall Place

Tracing the footsteps of major political figures and the city's industrial heritage, this walk (around 2.5 miles/4km and half a day) runs through the heart of everyday city life.

This route explores the area north of City Hall, a buzzing area where people work and shop. These streets are rich in stories of political figures, such as Henry Joy McCracken, and have witnessed the prosperity of many industries, from linen production and newspaper publishing to bootmaking and distilling. There are architectural delights that utilise the city's typical red sandstone, and the legacies of W. J. Barre and Charles Lanyon. City Hall is at the centre of Belfast life, both geographically and politically, and is the most appropriate place to start. At weekends, you'll often find political rallies outside its gates, concerning anything from trade union rights to the water quality of local loughs.

Highlights
- City Hall
- The Entries
- First Presbyterian Church
- Queen's Arcade
- Robinson & Cleaver

City Hall

This city of redbrick terraces and politico-historical folk is ruled from inside the marbled halls of Sir Brumwell Thomas's 1906 wedding-cake **City Hall** ❶ (Donegall Square; www.belfastcity.gov.uk/cityhall; free). City Hall dominates the commercial heart of Belfast. Conceived in response to Queen Victoria's award of city status to Belfast in 1888,

Open-top bus tours

Hop on, hop off open-top bus tours are a good way to see the city. Belfast City Sightseeing (www.belfastcitysightseeing.com) provides a comprehensive tour, beginning on Castle Place and taking in all the sights, including Titanic Belfast, the Botanic Gardens, St George's Market, Queen's University and the political and cultural murals splashed across the Falls and Shankill roads.

building began in 1898 on the site of the former White Linen Hall and took eight years to complete. Daily guided tours are free, and there is also a permanent, self-guided visitor exhibition on the journey of Belfast from past to present across sixteen rooms on the ground floor.

Once a symbol of unionist power, City Hall's Council Chamber saw an even split of nationalist and unionist councillors by its centenary year of 2006, thanks to Belfast's changing demographics. Along with the impressive visitor exhibition, the East Wing also features *The Bobbin Coffee Shop* (its name a nod to the linen industry) and toilet facilities (handy for tourists). Weddings take place at City Hall regularly and you'll more than likely spot a bridal party posing for photos on the grand staircase.

A debt to St Paul's

The City Hall's design, inspired by London's St Paul's Cathedral, has in turn provided inspiration with its Classical Renaissance style. It has a twin: Durban City Hall in South Africa, which was built in 1910. Like a giant wedding cake, a copper Ionic dome rises to 173ft (53 metres)

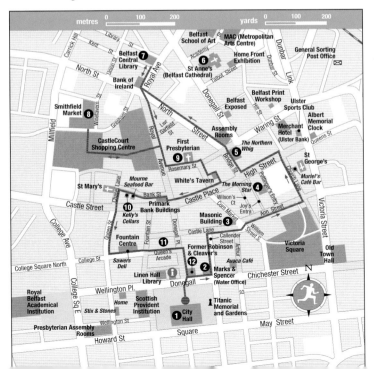

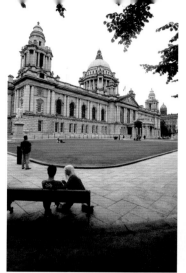

The copper-coated domes of City Hall.

Stained-glass windows inside City Hall trace Belfast's industrial past.

above the centre. Two storeys of a Portland stone quadrangle, each corner equipped with a tower, surround a central courtyard.

In front stands Thomas Brock's statue of Queen Victoria, unveiled by her son, King Edward VII, in 1903. She's accompanied by bronze figures that represent spinning, shipbuilding and education.

Inside, an ornate Carrara marble staircase sweeps up from the Entrance Hall to the Rotunda, colonnaded in Cipollino marble. Shooting off this are the Reception Room, Banqueting Hall and Council Chamber. Above the Rotunda, beneath the Great Dome, is the whispering gallery and John Luke's mural, commissioned to mark the 1951 Festival of Britain, illustrating the foundation of the city and the industries that provided its wealth. The striking Great Hall (rebuilt after

City Hall Gardens

Statues commemorate various worthies, from frock-coated mayors to James Magennis, a working-class Catholic from the Belfast slums who was the only Northern Ireland recipient of the Victoria Cross during World War II. The Belfast War Memorial is in the form of a cenotaph, while in the Titanic Memorial Garden, a plaque lists the name of each of the 1512 victims of the sinking of RMS *Titanic* in alphabetical order.

City Hall Gardens.

German bombing in 1941) retains its original seven stained-glass windows, depicting three monarchs who have visited Belfast (William III, Victoria and Edward VII), and the shields of Ireland's four provinces.

Grand architecture

Across Donegall Square North, east from the City Hall gates, the influence of Lanyon's firm crops up again in a red sandstone four-storey Venetian Gothic mass, completed in 1869 as a linen warehouse. This later became the Water Office until magisterially restored by **Marks & Spencer ❷**, the carved vegetable frieze suiting their business. On New Year's Day 1884, Oscar Wilde proclaimed this to be the city's sole beautiful building.

Beside M&S, and taking its name from callendering, a smoothing process for linen, Callender Street was once an alleyway for the businesses of distilling and newspaper publishing, now a short cut through to pedestrianised Castle Lane. Turn right on Castle Lane, where five streets converge on Arthur Square, at what is known as Corn Market, distinguished by its Spirit of Belfast steel sculpture of four interlocking rings, representing Belfast's linen and shipbuilding industries. Note the Art Nouveau detailing on the 1906 Mayfair Building and the 1870 **Masonic Building ❸**, at Nos. 13–21, also by Lanyon's firm and standing on the site of oyster houses, a trade that prospered down William Street South. Centuries

The decorative marble interior of City Hall.

Pottinger's Entry, the historical narrow alleyway.

back, Donegalls moored their pleasure barges in what is now Arthur Street, which branches out from here, and Corn Market was an active spot.

Highlights on Arthur Street include the stylish Irish homeware, clothes and gift shop Avoca, with its popular food hall and inviting café (see page 37), and Havana-style bar *Revolución de Cuba* (www.revoluciondecuba.com), housed in a delightfully restored Art Nouveau building.

Ann Street entries

In Ann Street, the 1798 Presbyterian leader Henry Joy McCracken was held at No. 13, before he was hanged in Corn Market (a place of public execution). Three of his fellow United Irishmen had already been executed and their heads displayed on spikes. Henry was spared beheading due to his families' standing.

However, our interest lies in nipping in and out of the quarter's narrow pub-lined entries, to your left heading north. From **Joy's Entry** (the third along), in 1737, McCracken's grandfather Francis Joy established what is now the oldest continuously

published newspaper in the English language, the *Belfast News Letter*. Its current rival, the *Irish News*, originally the *Morning News*, was first published in 1853 at No. 6 Crown Entry, the first entry you reach. The Society of United Irishmen was inaugurated in the *Crown Tavern* here in 1791. From **Wilson's Court**, between the two, the first edition of the United Irishmen's own newspaper, the *Northern Star*, was published.

Next, duck underneath a painted brick archway into **Pottinger's Entry** (see box), past the ornate **Morning Star ❹** where Mary Ann McCracken attempted to revive her brother, having first bribed the hangman. It is the last of the area's once-celebrated oyster houses. Still with its original facade and a wonderful horseshoe bar, it used to be a sailors' pub, at the start of the Dublin Coach route. Today, it's known for its old-school charm and as something of a journalists' and trade unionists' pub.

The acclaimed landscape watercolourist and printmaker Andrew Nicholl (1804–86) was a bootmaker's son from Church Lane, the next road

The Pottingers

Pottinger's Entry is named after a prominent local family who supplied the city with gold sovereigns and the British army with moustached majors. The most noted of the family was Sir Henry Pottinger, who as the first governor of Hong Kong successfully negotiated the British lease of Hong Kong after the Chinese Opium Wars. He died in retirement on the island of Malta, in 1856.

on the left. A blue plaque at No. 10 marks his birthplace. Next door is the quirky bohemian **Muriel's Café Bar** (tel: 028-9033 2445). A few doors down, at No. 4, is an atmospheric old tobacconist, Miss Moran Ltd, named after the woman who owned it from the 1930s to 1980s.

High Street and North Street

At the junction with High Street, glance across the road at the former National Bank – now an industrial-style bar and café *The National* (62 High Street) – where octagonal fish-scale turrets surmount a facade carved with centaurs and cornucopias. Turning west onto High Street, the tour traces the curve of the Farset River, which still flows beneath it. Here lived the McCracken family and Sir James Murray, the innovator of Milk of Magnesia.

As you make your way around High Street you'll see the *Ulster Sports Club* (96–98 High Street; www.ulster sportsclub.com), a hipster hangout with underground music gigs, club nights and its own Out of Office microbrewery and taproom.

Take a right into Bridge Street, past Arnott House, a grey 1950s abode sheltering a row of shops, which,

somewhat bafflingly, has been listed. Further on you'll spot the stylish **Northern Whig ❺** on the corner of Waring Street at one entrance to the Cathedral Quarter (see page 48). Dating from 1819, this cavernous listed building housed a hotel and newspaper offices (of the same name) before being converted into a popular bar, filled with dark wood and a warren of seating nooks.

Ahead is North Street, now sadly neglected with crumbling buildings and an air of abandonment. Plans for a regeneration development, announced in 2019, have so far come to nothing. On the corner of Lower Garfield Street stands Victorian tavern *The Deer's Head*. A two-minute detour through Writer's Square will bring you to **Belfast Cathedral, St Anne's ❻** (www.belfastcathedral.org), on Donegall Street, a glorious medley of mosaics, elaborate stonework and beautiful stained-glass windows.

Royal Avenue

Around the corner, Royal Avenue was the city's main shopping thoroughfare in the Victorian era. Here you will find the monumental red sandstone **Belfast**

Stopping for a pint at *The Morning Star*.

A colourful mural inside Smithfield Market.

Central Library ❼ (www.librariesni. org.uk; free). Designed by Lanyon's partner Lynn, after an architectural competition, it marked its 135th anniversary in 2023. For those wishing to research Belfast or Northern Irish history and culture, this is a good place to start, with a wide range of periodicals and newspapers dating back to the nineteenth century, plus free tours every Friday.

Next door stands the former office of the *Belfast Telegraph*, one of Northern Ireland's leading daily newspapers, which has moved to Clarendon Dock. Now known as simply The Telegraph Building, it hosts cultural events including chart-topping live bands and cutting-edge DJs.

Now, the route turns on its head to journey back down Royal Avenue towards Donegall Place and City Hall. Straddling the corner with North Street, you can't miss the old Bank of Ireland building. A fabulous example of Art Deco featuring a central clock, it is one of Belfast's finest buildings. Currently empty, it is slated to open

in 2028 as Belfast Stories, a vibrant community space that will share the stories of the city and her people, past, present and future, via exhibitions and social spaces.

The reflective glass and stainless steel of **Castle Court shopping centre** (www.castlecourt-uk.com) mirrors the confidence with which it was built (1988–1990). Until the 1960s this was the site of the original *Grand Central Hotel* (see page 19). The first floor now houses the luxurious Avenue Cinema, bar and café.

On Winetavern Street, at the back of Castle Court, **Smithfield Market** ❽ occupies the site of a famous Victorian market. Today, vendors sell a medley of goods, including comics, camping equipment and model soldiers. Retrace your steps through the shopping centre to Royal Avenue.

Rosemary Street

Our route diverts east into Rosemary Street where, in 1785, the celebrated actress Sarah Siddons performed at its long-gone eighteenth-century

TK Maxx) stands was once the Provost Prison where those to be hanged were held. Only W.H. Lynn's five-storey red sandstone **Bank Buildings**, now housing a large Primark store (destroyed by fire in 2018 but sympathetically restored and reopened in 2022), and the Victorian and Art Nouveau detail high up on Castle Buildings at Nos 8–18 Castle Place give a flavour of past times.

Next to Primark is 2 Royal Avenue (www.belfastcity.gov.uk), a former Victorian Bank of Ireland. It's a council-owned creative space with a café, children's play area, art exhibitions and, curiously, a grand piano. The building and interior have remained largely intact, so be sure to look up at its ornate circular dome.

A diversion

Tucked behind here, Bank Street runs west to **Kelly's Cellars** 🔟, a pub established in 1720 and retaining some of the conspiratorial ambiance generated when Henry Joy McCracken crouched beneath the counter escaping the Redcoats. A left turn leads to Chapel Lane opposite **St Mary's Roman Catholic Chapel**, whose walls date from 1783 and whose original opening was formally and ecumenically saluted by the Presbyterians of the First Company of

Playhouse, just opposite the historic **First Presbyterian Church** 🟑. Dating from 1781, this is the city's oldest surviving place of worship and the only church in Belfast with its own musician in residence. Pop in to see its ornate decor and boxed pews and you might catch a recital or practice session from a community ensemble or an Ulster Orchestra musician.

The route swerves right onto Lombard Street, where you'll see the 2023 statue honouring civil rights crusader and former enslaved American Frederick Douglass (1818–1895). He visited Belfast in 1846, giving speeches in favour of abolition, women's rights and temperance. Duck down Winecellar Entry to the atmospheric and photogenic **White's Tavern**, associated with the wine trade since 1630. A further right turn brings you back to High Street. Turn right again and head west into Castle Place, where little remains that would suggest its former Victorian commercial focus as a place of silk merchants and tea shops. Where the former Donegall Arcade (now home to

Fresh Garbage

Going to Fresh Garbage has been a teenage rite of passage since the alternative shop opened in 1969 on Bank Street. Now at 24 Rosemary Street (www.freshgarbage.co.uk), it's an absolute treasure trove for hippies, punks, goths, rockers and ravers, its shelves stocked with everything from incense sticks to vegan hair dye.

Belfast Volunteers. Cross Castle Street at the junction, with the 1865 *Hercules Bar* on the corner into Queen Street, and you'll stumble across a string of cheap-and-cheerful cafés and chain-owned coffee shops.

College Street to Donegall Place

At College Street, push east to find *Sawers* (5–6 Fountain Centre, College Street; www.sawersbelfast.com), established, and family owned, since 1897. It's a gourmand emporium, famous for its luxury hampers, imported delicacies and tempting deli bar with take-away sandwich baps such as the Belfast Buster, along with more than one hundred Irish and international cheeses.

Another local foodie favourite is *Jeffers Home Bakery* (4–6 College Street; www.jeffersbakery.co.uk), also family owned, and part of a chain of six across Co. Antrim. It's much loved for its cakes, traybakes and local speciality breads, such as soda and potato bread and the hearty Belfast Bap.

The 'Alice Clock' at the **Fountain Centre** is Ireland's only automaton clock, with a curious procession of characters from *Alice in Wonderland* and the Nativity.

Back on Fountain Street, soak up the atmosphere at one of its many bars and pubs, such as *Santería* (www.santeriabelfast.com) which serves up everything from coffee to Caribbean-themed cocktails; live rock music venue *Voodoo*; and popular drinking den *Fountain Lane*, which hosts traditional music sessions.

The listed, 1880s-built **Queen's Arcade** ⑪ is flanked by a handful of designer watch and jewellery shops. It's the last remaining Victorian arcade in Belfast and, in 2019, underwent a restoration to return it to its former glory. Back to the bustling Donegall Place your eyes will be drawn to eight maritime copper masts, installed in 2011 and now an established part of the cityscape. Each one represents a ship from the storied White Star Line, including RMS *Titanic*, built by Harland & Wolff.

Robinson & Cleaver

Donegall Place is now colonised almost entirely by British and European high-street multiples, but on its corner, opposite the City Hall, stands what was once the province's leading department store, still bearing the name of **Robinson & Cleaver** ⑫. Originally a linen warehouse, this six-storey monolith boasts a clock tower, a flock of Donatello cherubs, and fifty stone heads of those claimed as the firm's patrons, plus symbolic references to far-flung marketplaces. It opened for business in 1888 and shuttered in 1984, sadly not reaching its centenary. It now shelters a stylish restaurant, *Café Parisien* (www.cafeparisienbelfast.com) which offers lunch through to dinner, cocktails and a Sunday bottomless brunch.

Copper masts in Donegall Place.

Robinson & Cleaver.

Eating out

Avoca Café
41 Arthur Street; www.avoca.com.
Avoca's upstairs restaurant serves decent food that makes ample use of the island's ingredients, as well as the tasty home-baked goods for which the Irish brand is renowned. In the deli you can pick up takeaway lunches and foodie gifts. ££

Home
22 Wellington Place;
www.homebelfast.co.uk.
The philosophy here is fresh, local and seasonal with a range of vegan, vegetarian and gluten-free options alongside the more usual modern Irish offerings, such as fish, meat and game. The cocktail list combines old favourites as well as inspired classics-with-a-twist.

The Morning Star
17–19 Pottinger's Entry;
www.themorningstarbar.com.
A traditional pub, established in 1810, hidden down a narrow entry. Head up the steep staircase for a classic Belfast dining experience combining freshly, locally grown ingredients, with an emphasis on ethically reared grass-fed beef and steak. Herbs and vegetables are plucked straight from the venue's kitchen garden. ££

Mourne Seafood Bar
34–36 Bank Street;
www.mourneseafood.com.
Top of the list for seafood lovers. Fresh catch, sourced from the restaurant's shellfish beds, is cooked in a traditional style or with an Asian twist. The shellfish bar offers cheaper alternatives to the main menu, featuring small plates and, of course, a selection of oysters. £££

The Northern Whig
2–10 Bridge Street;
www.thenorthernwhig.com.
Formerly home to the newspaper of the same name, this bar and restaurant has been beautifully restored to provide an all-day dining spot on the edge of the Cathedral Quarter. The menu draws on cooking styles from around the world and offers light bites as well as main meals, comforting desserts and vegan options. ££

Stix & Stones
44–46 Upper Queen Street;
www.stixandstonesbelfast.co.uk.
The decor of this restaurant, which also has a branch in east Belfast, comprises chic stone and wood with rustic accents. Diners can cook their own steak or seafood on hot stones in a casual, laidback environment. ££

HISTORIC PUBS

Whether for its history, its *craic* or its decor, a visit to one of the atmospheric old pubs in Belfast should feature on every visitor's itinerary.

Belfast's population explosion in the eighteenth century meant that, by the time Queen Victoria came to the throne in 1837, there were 346 public houses. Today this profusion of pubs has dwindled but some of the old inns have survived and are worth seeking out for the wealth of history concealed behind their doors. Some bars now offer their own microbreweries; if you have time, try the craft-beer tour from Walking Tours Belfast (www.walking toursbelfast.com).

The craic

Spelled '*crack*' in traditional Ulster-Scots, the word was adopted by the Irish and Gaelicised in the mid-1960s as '*craic*', before being borrowed back into English. Whatever way you spell it, the meaning is the same: to have good fun, entertainment or conversation.

Pick of the best

McHugh's (29–31 Queen's Square; see page 67), in what is said to be Belfast's oldest building, dates from

Kelly's Cellars.

The Morning Star (www.the morningstarbar.co.uk; see page 37), hidden down Pottinger's Entry, at Nos. 17–19, this former terminal for the Belfast–Dublin mail coach has been beautifully restored.

Victorian gems

The jewel in the crown is the **Crown Liquor Saloon** (46 Great Victoria Street; www.nicholsonspubs.co.uk; see page 22), a stunning Victorian gin palace now owned by the National Trust. Built in the 1880s, it exhibits delightful craftsmanship, including exquisite tiling and stained glass. Look out, too, for the carved mahogany booths or snugs, built for drinkers who didn't necessarily want to be spotted. Opened in 1870, **The Garrick Bar** (29 Chichester Street; www.thegarrick bar.com) is a nicely restored pub, with gaslights outside and tiled floors inside.

Literary connections

The Duke of York (7–11 Commercial Court; www.dukeofyorkbelfast. com; see page 46) is known for many things, one of which is offering Northern Ireland's largest whiskey selection; another is for once employing former Sinn Féin leader Gerry Adams as bar staff. Antique memorabilia line the walls and ceilings, and outside, people take selfies beneath its Instagram-famous neon 'rain' sign and canopy of suspended umbrellas.

The John Hewitt (51 Donegall Street; www.boundarybrewing.coop; see page 46), named after the Belfast poet, is now run by a Belfast cooperative brewery, Boundary. **Bittles Bar** (70 Upper Church Lane; see page 67) is a distinctive drinking den thanks to its flat-iron shape and, inside, walls hung with pictures of Irish literary giants, from Wilde to Joyce.

1711. It has been skilfully renovated retaining some of the original features, including brickwork and exposed wooden beams, plus there's a ship's boiler built into the walls.

Established in 1720, **Kelly's Cellars** (30–32 Bank Street; www.kellys cellars.co.uk; see page 35) has live traditional music from Tuesday to Sunday. With its whitewashed walls, low arches and open fire, it feels like little has changed in two hundred years.

Claiming to be the city's oldest tavern, **White's Tavern** (2–4 Winecellar Entry; www.whitestavernbelfast. com; see page 35), tucked down a cobblestoned entry, was originally established in 1630. Its various extensions over the years include *The Tavern*, the *Beer Hall* and the *White's Store*, Ireland's first Guinness-only bar.

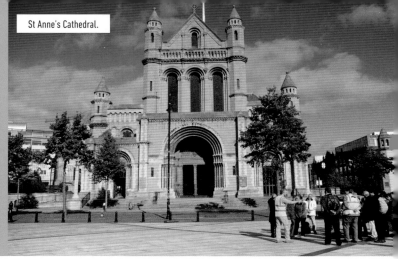

St Anne's Cathedral.

TOUR 3
Cathedral Quarter

At just over a mile (2km) and taking half a day, this short but sweet circular tour around the Cathedral Quarter is packed with history.

Cultural revival

The opening of the luxurious *Merchant Hotel* in 2006 gave a massive boost to Belfast's Cathedral Quarter, which features some of Belfast's oldest buildings and cobbled streets. By the 1990s, the area had fallen into disrepair and, given that a good proportion of its Victorian buildings remained, it was considered the best location to create a mixed artistic, commercial and entertainment enclave. The regeneration of this district is a huge success story, and it has become the hub of a thriving social scene. It stepped up another level in 2012 with the completion of the MAC (Metropolitan Arts Centre) along with a clutch of new restaurants and a hotel in Saint Anne's Square.

Highlights

- Royal Ulster Rifles Museum
- Merchant Hotel
- The MAC
- The Black Box
- Home Front Exhibition
- St Patrick's RC Church
- St Anne's Cathedral

Revitalised redbrick buildings shelter small galleries showcasing the work of photographers and installation artists. Potter around the tight network of cobbled streets and you will feel the modern vibe: old pubs rub shoulders with cool music venues, while hip cocktail bars and lauded restaurants are tucked down narrow alleyways.

Arts festival

Much of the success of the area in establishing a cultural identity has been down to a well-regarded alternative arts festival, the Cathedral Quarter Arts Festival (CQAF), which each May brings a wide variety of Irish and international artists to venues throughout the quarter.

Waring Street

We begin the route where Bridge Street meets Waring Street. Opposite the *Northern Whig* pub is a once-excellent, now-rundown building, the original 1769 Exchange and Assembly Rooms – simply known as the **Assembly Rooms**. In 1792 the premises hosted the famous Harp Festival, during which the young musicologist Edward Bunting transcribed the traditional airs and compositions of the last of this island's blind harpers. Later, in 1845, it was converted to a bank by Lanyon. It has been vacant since 2000 and is on the Heritage at Risk Register, its future currently uncertain.

After years of neglect, the lovely facade of the Four Corners building fronts a cookie-cutter *Premier Inn* hotel. Worth visiting on Waring Street, at No. 5, the **Royal Ulster Rifles Museum** ❶ (www.armymuseums.org.uk; free) has an extensive collection of regimental memorabilia and traces the regiment back to 1793.

Further on, a slight detour south to Skipper Street (which provided lodging for tea-clipper skippers) brings us to cosy, trendy bar, *The Spaniard*, at No. 3, which serves up excellent wine and tapas as well as a great selection of rums and cocktails.

Returning to Waring Street, on the corner is the Ulster Buildings, housing **The Cloth Ear** restaurant (see page 47), a solid 1869 sandstone block.

Opposite is the startling cubic frontage of a modern three-storey building on the site of a seventeenth-century pothouse. This was the site of William Waring's home, a tanner, after whom the street was named. His daughter, Jane, grew up to become Dean Jonathan Swift's "Varina", refusing to marry him while he was prebendary at Kilroot, near Carrickfergus, in 1696. It has gained a new lease of life as *The Thirsty Goat*, a lively bar and beer garden where you can dine on boxty (a traditional potato cake, served with toppings) while listening to live music.

Next door, Cotton Court is an old bonded warehouse. It is home to an eclectic mix, including the **Belfast Print Workshop** (www.bpw.org.uk), which provides facilities for artists in the field of printmaking to share ideas and create original works. The in-house gallery stocks a collection of their pieces. It also houses a whole host of other creatives including graphic designers and art consultants, and runs regular art classes, workshops and exhibitions. Peruse the huge tiled mural filling an entire wall and you will discover that it reflects the historic trades that were carried out in Waring

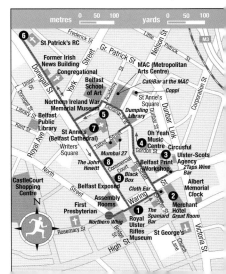

The sumptuous *Great Room* restaurant, in the *Merchant Hotel*, is situated in the former main Banking Hall of the building.

Street: tea merchants, saddlers, linen and damask manufacturers, millers, shirtmakers and marine engineering.

The Ulster-Scots Agency

The Ulster-Scots Agency (The Corn Exchange, 31 Gordon Street; www.ulsterscotsagency.com; free), housed in a historic 1852 building, promotes the cultural and linguistic links between Scotland and Ulster (just 13 miles apart), which continue to permeate Belfast and can be heard in numerous words and phrases, not least the ubiquitous descriptor 'wee'. The centre has a spacious gallery showcasing Ulster-Scots history, from the formation of the Giant's Causeway to the present day, and staff will supply you with ideas for day-trips out of the city to learn more. When former US president Barack Obama visited Belfast in June 2013 for the G8 summit in Northern Ireland, he was greeted at the international airport by a Stormont government minister with the words: 'Fair fae ye', meaning 'Welcome.'

Merchant Hotel

On the other side of the road stands the street's final distinctive building, the 1860s former Ulster Bank, now the **Merchant Hotel** ❷ (see page 125; 16 Skipper Street; www.the merchanthotel.com), encircled by an elaborate cast-iron balustrade and etched with an extravaganza of Thomas Fitzpatrick's carvings. The skyline is dominated by his figures of Britannia, Justice and Commerce, and urns surmount the corners. The Grade A-listed building was bought and restored at enormous cost by Beannchor, which runs various Belfast restaurants and bars. It opened in 2006 as the *Merchant*, and quickly established itself as one of Northern Ireland's premier luxury hotels.

The hotel radiates wealth, not least in the spectacular **Great Room** restaurant (see page 47), where Ireland's largest chandelier hangs beneath a glass cupola. It's a desirable spot for afternoon tea. Elsewhere, there's a luxury spa and rooftop gym with panoramic views of the city. *Bert's Jazz Bar* is also a fashionable spot for authentic live jazz in Art Deco surroundings.

The MAC

The MAC (Metropolitan Arts Centre, St Anne's Square; www.themaclive.com; free), which opened in 2012, is Belfast's cutting-edge cultural venue. It comes with two theatres, three art galleries and artists' studios, along with a café, bar and restaurant. With its redbrick and dark basalt, as well as oak furnishings, Danish fabric panels, steel balustrades and bronze window frames, it has caught the imagination of locals and visitors alike.

Hill Street

Diagonally opposite the hotel, with its many hidden courtyards (their corners protected from carriage wheels by heavy iron bollards) and some listed brick and stucco warehouses, the cobblestoned **Hill Street** typifies the promise that earned the area its regeneration. At Nos. 18–22 the **Black Box** (www.blackboxbelfast.com) stages live music, drama, club nights, comedy, exhibitions, science festivals, cabaret and more. It also offers guided street art walking tours of the Cathedral Quarter.

Just off Hill Street on the right, at 23–25 Gordon Street, is one of the quarter's more unusual stars, **Circusful** ❸ (www.circusful.org), formerly the **Belfast Community Circus,** housed in a suitably brightly coloured building. Classes are available for budding performers aged upwards of two years. Its band of accomplished artistes perform throughout the year, from special days at St George's Market to numerous City Council events and at the venue's cabaret nights. Biggest of all is its own Festival of Fools in May, with trapeze artists, acrobats and wire walkers in action on the streets.

Staying on Gordon Street, at Nos. 15–21 is the **Oh Yeah Music Centre** ❹ (www.ohyeahbelfast.com; free), named after the 1996 song from Downpatrick-band Ash. This converted warehouse hosts a permanent music exhibition charting the history of local music, from trad folk to Snow Patrol, and its assorted figures, including Van Morrison. There's also a rehearsal space, café, bar and recording studio, as well as events such as an 'acoustic picnic' with activities for children, food and live music. Return to Hill Street and continue to the end.

Looking out over the atrium at the MAC.

The glistening steel spire of St Anne's Cathedral.

Saint Anne's Square

Divert left to visit the **Northern Ireland War Memorial Museum** ❺ (www.niwarmemorial.org; free) at 21 Talbot Street, which gives an in-depth account of Northern Ireland during World War II, telling the story of the Belfast Blitz of 1941, which killed more than 1100 people and damaged 53 percent of the city's housing stock. There are also displays on the Ulster Home Guard, wartime industry and the American presence via photos, artefacts and interactive exhibits.

Oh Yeah Music Centre.

Return to Hill Street now and cross over to **Saint Anne's Square**, which runs behind the Protestant Belfast Cathedral of St Anne (also known as St Anne's Cathedral). The highlight of this neo-Palladian development is the MAC, Northern Ireland's flagship home for the arts (see page 43). Surrounding the square are blocks of smart porticoed apartments sitting alongside half a dozen trendy restaurants serving everything from modern Irish and Italian to contemporary Asian cuisine.

Back to Donegall Street

Leaving the pleasing rear view of the 1901 cathedral building on the left, cross the square in front of the £364-million redevelopment of the Belfast School of Art at Ulster University's Belfast campus, completed in 2022. The street here is known as **Academy Street**, so-called after David Manson's 1768 co-educational establishment. Despite regulations forbidding dogs and guns, in the eighteenth century nine pupils took their masters hostage at gunpoint at No. 2 (now demolished but once the Belfast Academy) when they heard Easter Holidays were to be cancelled. No. 40, built as a distiller's warehouse, now houses the Belfast Education and Library Board. Join up with Donegall Street and head northwest up towards St Patrick's Church. At No. 90 stands **The Kremlin** (www.kremlin-belfast.com), one of Belfast's most popular and best-known LGBTQ+ venues, with three separate levels, themed nights, drag shows and a legendary nightclub. On the opposite side of the road, down from the former *Irish News* offices (now relocated to the Fountain Centre, College Street), is a 1932 reconstruction of the German Blitz-damaged 1860 sandstone of **Donegall Street Congregational Church**.

Financing St Patrick's

In the early nineteenth century, Catholics accounted for one-sixth of Belfast's population and numbers mushroomed as people flocked to the city to work in the new industries. A plot of ground was leased in 1809 from the marquis of Donegall for a new church. Of the £4100 raised to finance St Patrick's construction, £1300 was subscribed by Protestants – an indication that the two communities were not always at each other's throats.

St Patrick's

John Willis, first organist at the 1815 Gothic Revivalist (rebuilt in 1877) **St Patrick's Roman Catholic Church** ❻ beyond, was dismissed almost as soon as he was engaged for playing variations on *The Boyne Water*, a belligerent Orange Protestant marching tune, at a service. The side chapel triptych of St Patrick, the Madonna and St Bridget is by the society painter and war artist Sir John Lavery. The Madonna's face is that of Lavery's wife Hazel, said by her husband to have influenced her friend, Irish revolutionary Michael Collins, to sign the Anglo-Irish treaty of 1921 that ushered in partition.

Next to the church, St Patrick's School, 1828, was the first Catholic school to be built in Belfast. The elegant three-storey houses to the north have since been carefully restored, making them among the earliest block of domestic premises to survive in the city.

St Anne's Cathedral

Retrace your steps south to the main facade of **St Anne's Cathedral (Belfast Cathedral)** ❼. Pause here and reflect on **Writers' Square** opposite, a public

The exterior of St Patrick's Roman Catholic Church.

space popular with skateboarders, which contains sculptural pieces by John Kindness and Brian Connolly. It is also used as a venue for street performers and festival events, including the Festival of Fools and the Cathedral Quarter Arts Festival.

A neo-Romanesque construction of Portland stone, begun in 1898, St Anne's Cathedral only added its stainless-steel spire in 2007 (see page 45). It succeeds a previous parish church, named as much after Anne – wife of the fifth earl of Donegall – as after Mary's mother. The rather plain nave's spaciousness is due in part to

View from the spire

In 2007 a futuristic 131ft (40m) stainless-steel spire, known as the Spire of Hope, was installed on the top of Belfast's St Anne's Cathedral. If you stand in the choir stalls, you can look up and see the heavens (as long as it's not one of Belfast's many cloudy days). Illuminated at night, it has become a significant landmark on the Belfast skyline.

The Cloth Ear.

it being built around its predecessor, where services were held until 1903. The pulpit, designed by Gilbert Scott, was carved by Harry Hems. Impressive features include a tympanum filled with a mosaic of angel musicians on a background of gold, one of Ireland's largest church organs, and delightful stained-glass windows. The baptistery has an incredible ceiling made of

Inside St Anne's Cathedral.

150,000 pieces of glass, representing the basic elements of creation. In 2012, as part of the Titanic centennial commemorations, an elegant *Titanic* Funeral Pall was unveiled.

The rest of Donegall Street

Push south down Donegall Street to one of Belfast's most culturally lively pubs, the cooperatively run **John Hewitt** ❽ (www.boundarybrewing. coop) at No. 51. Named after a famous local poet (1907–1987), it maintains a vibrant atmosphere and is the stomping ground of writers and musicians. It is a hub of activity during festival time.

Just off Donegall Street is cobbled Commercial Court (which we saw from the other end on Hill Street). Here, the *Duke of York* (www.duke ofyorkbelfast.com) was a hacks' pub where Gerry Adams, former president of Sinn Féin, worked behind the bar in the 1960s. Today it's better known for its selection of whiskey and, outside in the alley, photo-friendly neon arch and hanging umbrellas.

Back on Donegall Street, No. 23 conceals **Belfast Exposed** ❾ (tel: 028-9023 0965), Northern Ireland's first dedicated photography gallery, which has a large archive of digital images. It includes the offices of the annual Belfast Film Festival (www.belfastfilmfestival. org), which takes place in April, with a programme of premieres, classics and short-film competitions. The Visions Studio also has a calendar of digital screenings throughout the year. Northern Visions (www.nvtv.co.uk), a community media and arts project that broadcasts a local TV channel, is also based here.

Continue to the end of Donegall Street and you arrive back at the start of the walk.

Belfast's Cathedral Quarter.

Eating out

2Taps Wine Bar
Cotton Court, 30–42 Waring Street; www.2taps-winebar.co.uk.
A taste of Spain in the heart of Belfast. Relax in the inviting dining room or eat alfresco on the heated outdoor terrace. Meat, fish and vegetarian tapas, fresh salads and paella made to order are among the Spanish specialities. ££

CaféBar at the MAC
10 Exchange Street West; www.themaclive.com.
An ideal pit stop on your cultural tour of Belfast's largest arts venue. The all-day menu includes a seasonal salad bowl, tacos and signature breakfast and brunch sandwiches. Vegan and vegetarian options are also on the menu. £

The Cloth Ear
Merchant Hotel, 16 Skipper Street; www.themerchanthotel.com.
A good all-round menu that changes regularly to reflect the seasons, with a decent selection of plant-based options. The space is roomy, and many tables are big enough to cater for larger groups. ££

Coppi
St Anne's Square; www.coppi.co.uk.
This contemporary restaurant is named after Fausto Coppi, an Italian cyclist from the mid-twentieth century. Feast on *cichetti* (Venetian tapas) washed with a glass of Prosecco, antipasti sharing boards or delicious *pizzettas*. For a more substantial dish, try the pasta which is made daily in the kitchen. ££

Dumpling Library
St Anne's Square; www.dumplinglibrary.co.uk.
Part of the popular Zen restaurant group, this buzzing pan-Asian restaurant is a great haunt for quality cocktails as well as small sharing plates, influenced by traditional Chinese, Korean and Japanese flavours. ££

Great Room
Merchant Hotel, 16 Skipper Street; www.themerchanthotel.com.
Prepare to be blown away by the splendid dining room, with its original Victorian interior set beneath a glass cupola. Luckily, the menu lives up to the decor: classic dishes are given an innovative spin, using local ingredients. Also a good bet for scrumptious afternoon tea. Recommended for special occasions. £££

OX
1 Oxford Street; www.oxbelfast.com.
Upon opening in 2013, *OX* quickly scooped the accolade of Belfast's best fine-dining experience from critics and diners alike. Its no-choice tasting menu is packed with fresh, local ingredients brought to life by the talented chef-owner, while the wine list is equally well thought through. £££

The Crescent Arts Centre.

TOUR 4
Queen's Quarter

Based around Sir Charles Lanyon's Queen's University, this 2-mile (3km) half-day walk is a mixture of student haunts, elegant academia and designer stores.

A once genteel area, and one of Belfast's more rewarding for fans of Victorian and Edwardian architecture, the **Queen's Quarter** is also peppered with has lively student pubs, restaurants, art galleries, boutique hotels and budget hostels, as well as one of Belfast's best-known roads for high-end fashion labels. The autumnal Belfast International Arts Festival, hosted by Queen's University until 2015 and now run independently, makes an excellent introduction to the city for the first-time visitor as it utilises so many venues around Belfast.

Bradbury Place

Start in Bradbury Place, just south of Shaftesbury Square, where during the 1950s and 1960s **Lavery's ❶** (Nos.

Highlights
- Crescent Arts Centre and Gardens
- Lisburn Road shops
- Queen's University
- Ulster Museum
- Botanic Gardens

12–18; www.laverysbelfast.com) was a haven for artists and poets, including William Conor, John Hewitt and Louis MacNeice. In the 1970s it welcomed punk and has been home to various youth cultures ever since. Today, the three-storey hangout offers a wide range of live music throughout the week, from alternative rock to folk. A labyrinth of bars includes the 22-table pool room that opens out

Shop till you drop

Along the second half of the 2-mile (3.2km) length of Lisburn Road, between Adelaide Park and Maryville Park, you will find more than one hundred independent businesses providing a wide range of shops, from designer-filled boutiques to art galleries, antique stores and contemporary homeware studios, complemented by a variety of restaurants, bars and delis to satiate hunger pangs.

The Crescents

Further south, past an octagonal Art Deco weathercock-topped building at No. 48 and over the railway bridge, into the University Conservation Area, the 1873 Scrabo stone baronial pile that is the **Crescent Arts Centre ❷** (2–4 University Road; www.crescentarts.org), stands at the corner of University Road and Lower Crescent. This maze of rooms and studios plays host to a huge variety of regular workshops and classes in all aspects of the arts, from creative writing to dance, and hosts regular live events as well as the annual Belfast Book Festival each June (www.belfastbookfestival.com).

The neighbouring **Crescent Church** is evangelical in its worship and French medieval in its architectural inspiration. Our route nips east behind the church past the grand pilasters of the stuccoed Georgian

onto the rooftop beer gardens, and newest addition, *The Woodworkers*, which serves specialist craft beer.

At No. 10 Bradbury Place is *Darcy's* (www.darcysbelfast.co.uk), a family-run restaurant with a great Irish soda bread starter. Across the road at Nos. 23–31 is *Alibi* (www.alibibelfast.com), a nightclub, cocktail bar and grill over three levels. At Nos. 7–21, *Benedicts of Belfast* (www.benedictshotel.co.uk) is a four-star hotel with a buzzy bar, live music on some nights, and a restaurant.

A lengthy detour from Bradbury Place, taking the right fork along the long Lisburn Road (see box), will, after a twenty-minute walk, take dedicated shoppers to one of Belfast's prime districts for independent boutiques and art galleries, interspersed with great places to eat; it's a hive of activity.

At the junction of Lisburn Road and Bradbury Place is tiny **King William Park**, commemorated in Frank Ormsby's eponymous ironic poem, where William III hitched his horse in 1690. Note the pinnacle spire of the 1887 Moravian church and the campanile of the Wesleyan chapel, designed by W. J. Barre, which would not look out of place in Lombardy.

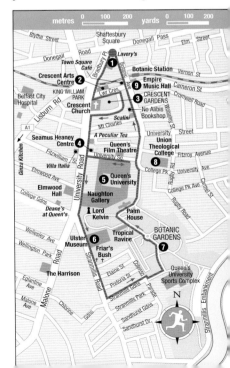

The Lanyon Building at Queen's University.

terraces of Lower Crescent and the pleasant **Crescent Gardens** ❸ (once a potato patch). At No. 13 is one of the city's earliest boutique hotels, formerly the *Crescent Townhouse*, now rebranded and relaunched as *The 1852* (www.the1852.com) with contemporary interiors and custom-made furniture and fittings. Its excellent *Town Square* café (45 Botanic Avenue; www.townsquarebelfast.com) has a casual vibe, serving breakfast until late – perfect for a lazy Saturday morning catch-up over eggs Benedict and hand-roasted coffee. In the evenings, it's a pleasant spot for a relaxed candlelit dinner.

University Road

Returning to imposing Upper Crescent and then University Road, we pass southwards to the pleasant stucco and Doric porticoes of Mount Charles, once home to novelist Forrest Reid and the poet John Hewitt.

Along University Road is a scattering of eateries, ranging from *A Peculiar Tea*'s five-course tasting menu and afternoon tea (see box), to the ever-popular pizzeria restaurant **Villa Italia** (see page 54). Turn into Elmwood Avenue to find *The Parlour* at Nos. 2–4 (www.parlourbar.co.uk).

This 1930s-themed student bar serves tasty pizza and hosts live music.

Across the road are three Georgian rows, Prospect Terrace, Botanic View and Cinnamon Buildings, plus the Victorian stucco and Georgian brick terraces of Camden and Fitzwilliam streets. These, respectively, were the home ground of Brian Moore's 1956 novel, *The Lonely Passion of Judith Hearne*, and the site of Nobel Laureate poet Seamus Heaney's campus flat.

Take a detour east down Georgian University Square to view a string of houses – now university departments – that sport magnolia in their gardens. Also worth a visit is the **Seamus Heaney Centre** ❹ (www.qub.ac.uk), attached to the School of English at Queen's and a regular venue for literary talks and events of a consistently high calibre. In 2024 it is due to relocate to Nos. 38–40 University Road nearby. At 20 University Square is the **Queen's Film Theatre**, a home for independent, arthouse and world cinema (www.queensfilmtheatre.com). It has two big screens, a theatre and a comfortable bar and lounge in which to debate the relative merits of Yasujirō Ozu and Quentin Tarantino.

Back on University Road, The Church of Ireland's Canon Hannay

(1865–1950), aka George A. Birmingham, the nationalistic author of sixty-plus satirical novels, lived at No. 75; painter Paul Henry lived at No. 61.

Queen's University

Charles Lanyon designed the pleasingly mellowed redbrick facade of **Queen's University** ❺ (see box), shamelessly appropriating the lines of the Founder's Tower at Magdalen College, Oxford, for its central feature. The university was named after the young Victoria when she laid the foundation stone in 1845.

The first students were all young men; women were only allowed to enrol in arts classes from 1882 onwards, with science following in 1883 and medicine in 1889. Adhering to the hierarchical nature of the times, the architect provided lavish accommodation for chancellors and other dignitaries while offering the students little except for four water closets and a row of urinals. Happily, the new off-campus student villages now compensate for this.

It's worth picking up the *Campus Walkabout Guide* leaflet from the Queen's Welcome Centre to help you on a signposted tour; enter the university's main gates and follow signs for the welcome centre. In particular, seek out the Great Hall, which Lanyon based on the medieval great halls of the Oxbridge universities. Also check out the **Naughton Gallery** (www.naughtongallery.org; free) in the Lanyon Building, which houses the university's own art collection and often hosts touring exhibitions. The **Brian Friel Theatre** (www.qub.ac.uk), named in honour of one of Ireland's most illustrious playwrights, is located at No. 20 University Square.

Queen's campus

Queen's University campus is modest in size and, so, as the university expanded to its present numbers of 25,000 students and 2000-plus teaching and research staff, it began buying up vacant buildings in the area. Currently, the university estate comprises more than 250 buildings, of which 98 are listed. A large proportion of students come from Northern Ireland, and many go home to their families at weekends, so social activities are less exuberant than one might expect.

Elegant room at *The Harrison*.

Sculpture outside the Ulster Museum.

Opposite the university's lawns is the One Elmwood Student Centre, home to the Students' Union. It opened in September 2022, after the former building was replaced by this £42m state-of-the-art space. There is also Elmwood Hall, a former Presbyterian church, above whose three-tiered spire a gilt weathercock basks in the sun. At No. 28 is the Catholic Chaplaincy where the poet Philip Larkin (1922–85) wrote many of his finest lines during his five years working as a librarian at Queen's University. Back on University Road,

past Methodist College on the right, the road divides into Malone and Stranmillis, the former a middle-class expanse of leafy avenues.

At 45 Malone Road, opposite the *Post House* bar, you'll find *The Harrison* (www.chambersofdistinction. com), one of the city's most stylish boutique hotels. It shelters within an impressive four-storey terrace of former apartments, nicknamed Batchelors' Row in the 1930s – a nod to the wealthy, well-educated young men who lived there.

Ulster Museum

Our route now enters the gates of the Botanic Gardens by the 1912 **statue to Lord Kelvin**, formulator of the Second Law of Thermodynamics.

The landmark architecture of the **Ulster Museum ❻** (www.ulster museum.org; free) is remarkable for the 1972 Brutalist extension to its 1929 Classical Revival original wing. The museum features a 75ft (23m) -high glass-and-steel atrium, known as 'Window on Our World', that directs you to the history, art and nature zones. In the spectacular rooftop gallery, the glass, jewellery and Belleek collections are shown off to their very best.

World of discovery

With engaging displays, hands-on areas and a range of interactive programmes, a visit to the Ulster Museum will provide kids with a stimulating learning experience. There are all sorts of cool things for young ones to discover: how big were dinosaurs? Want to see real treasure that was lost at sea? Or meet an ancient Egyptian mummy? Well, now you can. The explorer map and stickers are free of charge, available from the welcome area.

Everyone is an artist at the Ulster Museum.

The splendid Botanic Gardens and Palm House.

Beside the museum at 12 Stranmillis Road is the atmospheric **Friar's Bush** walled graveyard – thought to be Belfast's oldest Christian burial ground. It contains a mass grave of cholera victims and the mysterious Friar's Stone with the date AD485 inscribed on it (some people doubt the relic's authenticity).

Botanic Gardens

South of the Ulster Museum, Stranmillis Gardens leads back into the **Botanic Gardens** ❼ (www.belfast city.gov.uk/botanicgardens; free) where a northwestern course through hedged walks leads to both the **Tropical Ravine** and the **Palm House**. The original ravine, dating from 1889, reopened in 2018 after a sympathetic (and energy-efficient) restoration. Some of the plants, split over two levels in a miniature sunken rainforest, are said to be more than 150 years old. Palm fronds form exotic patterns against the glass dome, which was completed in 1840 by ironmaster Richard Turner (before he built the Great Palm House at Kew Gardens), to Lanyon's designs. The gardens often hold events, including Belfast's annual Indian festival, Mela

(www.belfastmela.org.uk). There is also a children's playground for the little ones to let off some steam.

Beyond the Palm House, the north gate leads on to College Park and Botanic Avenue, while an optional diversion via the east gate takes you first through a district of neat redbrick terraces and a profligacy of churches, known as the Holy Land because so many of its street names derive from biblical cities.

Ahead, on Botanic Avenue, the formidable Scrabo stone mass of the **Union Theological College** ❽ is fronted by a colonnaded facade by Lanyon. Persuasive charm may gain you entry to the impressive – also colonnaded – domed library, used by Northern Ireland's House of Commons while it awaited Stormont's completion. Its Senate sat in the chapel.

Botanic Avenue

The houses of Botanic Avenue retain, on their second and third floors, evidence of their 1870s origins. Deemed Belfast's Boul' Mich' (Boulevard St Michel in Paris) by Nobel Prize-winning poet Seamus Heaney (1939–2013), it once carried itself with a raffish louche air, but is now slightly more down at heel, its tree-lined pavements fronting on to charity shops, fast-food outlets and vape shops.

A few places well worth checking out include *Maggie Mays* café at No. 50, which serves a budget-friendly, home-cooked menu (www.maggie maysbelfast.com); the fantastic crime-specialist bookshop at No. 83, No Alibis (www.noalibis.com) with literary readings and book launches;

at No. 85, the jovial Italian restaurant *Scalini* (see page 54); and at Nos. 59–63 the *House Belfast* hotel (www.housebelfast.co.uk), with its eye-catching facade.

The atmospheric **Empire Music Hall** ❾ (www.belfastempire.com) – housed in a deconsecrated church – provides live music and stand-up comedy as well as a lively bar. Go past Kinghan Mission Church now, and you will find yourself back at Shaftesbury Square where we began.

Eating out

A Peculiar Tea
44 University Road;
www.a-peculiar-tea.com.
A labour of love from chef Gemma Austin, this quirky addition to the food scene around Queen's embraces playfulness through its afternoon teas and creatively themed set menus inspired by everything from children's books to Broadway. Sustainability is another passion, and the kitchen operates a no-waste policy. £££

Deanes at Queens
1 College Gardens;
www.michaeldeane.co.uk.
From the stable of renowned local restauranteur Michael Deane, *Deanes at Queens* brings contemporary sophistication and a continental style of eating using local, in-season food prepared in stylish ways. Lunches offer good value if the evening menu is out of your price range. An alfresco eating area overlooks the leafy College Gardens. £££

Ginza Kitchen
245 Lisburn Road;
www.ginzabelfast.com.
A fantastic and varied selection of Japanese food in friendly, relaxed surroundings. The sushi is a hit here, the cocktails delicious and the

vegetarian and kids' options have been well thought through. ££

Scalini
85 Botanic Avenue;
www.scalinirestaurant.co.uk.
A Tuscan-inspired *trattoria* with an extensive menu covering Italian classics as well as dishes with a hint of Northern Ireland. ££

Town Square
45 Botanic Avenue;
www.townsquarebelfast.com.
Town Square café is part of *The 1852* hotel with a simple menu featuring burritos, tacos, ciabatta sandwiches and burgers, as well as breakfast and brunch dishes, all complemented by a convivial, relaxed atmosphere. The adjoining bar serves cocktails, craft beer and an impressive selection of gins. ££

Villa Italia
39–41 University Road;
www.villaitaliarestaurant.co.uk.
A warm and welcoming family-run pizzeria. Interiors are rustic Italian with murals on the walls, terracotta tiles on the floor and grapevines hanging from the ceiling. The list of pizzas is extensive, so too the antipasti and pasta dishes but do leave room for the desserts. ££

TOUR 5
City meets the waterfront

This 2.5-mile (4km) half-day stroll revolves around the waterfront from Lanyon Place to Clarendon Dock and the streets behind to discover Belfast's seafaring history.

Belfast has a long maritime history that has become an integral part of the city's growing tourist industry. Following years of neglect, the Laganside Corporation was set up in 1989, and by attracting large levels of investment into the waterfront, successfully transformed the area. A smart promenade provides easy access, and development has subsequently spread to the docks area. Our tour also takes you behind the waterfront to see statues, monuments and other memorabilia, mostly associated with Belfast's watery past.

Highlights
- St George's Market
- Waterfront Hall
- Albert Memorial Clock
- Custom House
- Big Fish
- Sinclair Seamen's Presbyterian Church

Around City Hall

It may seem a little strange to begin this waterfront-themed walk at **City Hall** (see page 28), but it is here in the hall's grounds that you'll find the **Titanic Memorial ❶**. The *Titanic* was built in Belfast, and the city's shipbuilding heritage is further honoured by the annual Belfast Maritime Festival, with its displays, exhibitions and flotilla of vessels and ships in Queen's Quay and the Abercorn Basin (see page 68).

Spoilt for choice at St George's Market.

At the memorial's base, two weeping sea-nymphs break the sea's cold grasp at the feet of a scantily clad marble statue of a female Fame, in their arms the RMS *Titanic*'s Unknown Soldier, an anonymous drowned man. An inscription in gold leaf records the

The Titanic Memorial in the grounds of City Hall.

names of eleven 'gallant Belfast men who lost their lives on 15 April 1912 by the foundering of the Belfast-built RMS *Titanic* through collision with an iceberg, on her maiden voyage from Southampton to New York'. But there is no mention of the dozens of doomed Belfast-born artisan crew and steerage-class passengers – or indeed of any women – on board. The eleven gallant men comprised the shipyard's Guarantee Group, which was checking performance targets on the vessel's maiden voyage. In 2012, a granite memorial listing the names of every person who died in the tragedy was unveiled in a new **Titanic Memorial Garden**.

Nearby, an aggressive bronze figure in a pith helmet and puttees serves as an 1899–1902 **Boer War cenotaph**. The rock on which he stands is, as was the custom of the times, supported by two bare-breasted and two flimsily covered goddesses.

Opposite, at Nos. 11–13 Donegall Square East, is a hexastyle Corinthian

Secret marriage

May Street is named after the May family, who married Anna, an illegitimate daughter, to the second marquis of Donegall. Although they became sovereigns of the city, the snobbish marquis kept the marriage a secret.

porticoed facade, all that remains of the original once-grand 1840s Methodist church. Its congregation long gone to the suburbs, its 1500-seat auditorium transferred from God to Mammon and its fine box pews cannibalised for pubs and restaurants, it has been rebuilt as the Ulster Bank's corporate headquarters. Harry Ferguson designed the minimal-maintenance Ferguson tractor, revolutionising British farming, at Nos. 14–16. Other nineteenth-century shipbuilders lived at Nos. 18–20. From Donegall Square East, push east down May Street to the waterfront.

May Street

A great linen warehouse by Lanyon once stood at the top of May Street, the longest street in the city centre, on the right. Another Lanyon creation, originally the Church of Ireland Diocesan offices, in polychrome brick, still stands opposite.

The provocative Reverend Henry Cooke preached in May Street's 1859 classically designed **Presbyterian Church ❷**. He refused Temperance meetings and gave serious consideration to a proposal to use its basement cemetery as a bonded whiskey warehouse. Nowadays, the church is run by Central Belfast, a city-centre church under the auspices of Carnmoney Presbyterian Church, with the congregation amalgamated with Fisherwick Church on Malone

Road. These changes aside, the building's impressive twin staircases, box pews, mahogany gallery and timber-coffered ceiling remain.

To its east, towards the river, are the Doric columns of the church school. Almost opposite, Victoria Hall stands on the site of the Victoria Music Hall where, in 1882, a cornice fell, narrowly missing the novelist Charles Dickens while he was delivering a reading. The music hall was demolished in 1983; what stands in its place, Victoria Hall, is an office building.

Auctioneers Ross & Co occupy the souk-like caverns of Nos. 22–26, built in attractive brick and sandstone as the Presbyterian General Assembly's

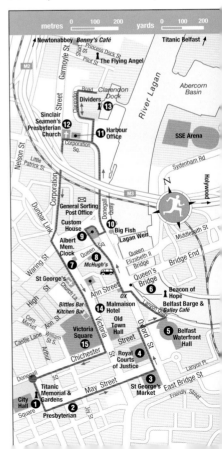

Office in 1875. Veterinary surgeon John Boyd Dunlop invented the first successful pneumatic tyre at Nos. 38–42 and ran a hospital for sick horses where Telephone House now stands.

St George's Market

Beyond, on the corner with Verner Street, stands *Ronnie Drews*. Renamed after one of the mainstays of the famous Dubliners folk band, this cosy drinking den hosts traditional Irish music sessions, as well as DJ and singer-songwriter nights. The brick, stone and iron Market House (1890), sympathetically restored to the original designs as **St George's Market** ❸ (www.belfastcity.gov. uk/stgeorgesmarket; free), is all that remains of many such markets that peppered the Laganside end of May Street, in an area still known colloquially as The Markets.

St George's is the oldest covered market in Belfast. With the growing popularity of farmers' markets and natural produce, it has become a must-visit, as much for the building's fine architecture as for the goods. Alongside groceries, there are hot food stands offering global treats such as

Home-made scones for sale at St George's Market.

gourmet burgers, paella and dhals, and live-music sets in the afternoons. Local artists, photographers, craftspeople and artisan makers sell great gifts to bring home.

On the first floor is the award-winning *Stock Kitchen & Bar* (www.stockbelfast.com) from chef Danny Millar. The kitchen works

St George's Market

St George's Market (Fri 8am–2pm, Sat 9am–3pm, Sun 10am–3pm) has become a genuine draw for foodies with all kinds of (mainly Northern Irish) produce, from cheeses, chutneys and cupcakes to a wide range of freshly caught fish and seafood, organic meats from local farmers, and speciality breads. Besides the food, there's also an eclectic mix of craft, book and antique stalls and displays of works by local artists, photographers and jewellery-makers.

Local organic vegetables.

Night falls over Belfast Waterfront Hall.

with local suppliers, including some of the market's own traders, and you'll find the names of specific farms and fisheries listed on the menu. If you're lucky to nab a seat on the dining balcony, you can watch the marketplace bustle below.

The open kitchen adds a touch of theatre to proceedings.

Royal Courts of Justice

Across May Street, west through iron security gates at the bottom of Chichester Street, stands the imposing Neoclassical bulk of the **Royal Courts of Justice** ❹. Bewigged barristers and pinstriped solicitors parade, clutching pink-ribboned legal bundles, while miscreants, plaintiffs and their accusers and pursuers seem (mostly) in awe of the travertine marble vastness of the echoing central hall. Opposite is the Old Town Hall, completed in 1870, and now a Grade B1-listed building. After suffering both minor (the Blitz) and major (the IRA) bomb damage it was restored and used as a county court until 2020. It is currently vacant.

On the waterfront

Opposite, in what is now Lanyon Place, where noisy, vibrant markets once thrived, dealing in the likes of cattle, flax, fruit, grain, horse, pork, potato, fish and all kinds of other local goods, are the spare, sandy-coloured towers of the *Hilton Hotel*, a car park and the BT building.

The towering buildings of Lanyon Place (see page 60) almost dwarf the stylishly emblematic **Belfast Waterfront Hall** ❺

Take an evening stroll along the waterfront.

(www.waterfront.co.uk) whose striking copper dome has sadly been largely obscured from the roadside by subsequent surrounding soulless multi-storey developments.

Belfast's most prestigious concert venue after the nearby SSE Arena, it regularly draws major rock and pop acts and is also worth checking for drama, ballet, opera and musicals. Cross to the waterfront and head downstream, north towards **Queen's Bridge ❻**. Designed by Charles Lanyon and named after Queen Victoria, the bridge was built of Newry granite to replace the old Long Bridge, which had been *the* place in 1790 for an evening's *paseo*.

At the corner of Queen's Bridge, in what is now Thanksgiving Square, visitors can enjoy the *Beacon of Hope*. Created by Scottish artist Andy Scott, and constructed in 2007, the 64ft (19.5m) stainless steel and bronze statue depicts a girl standing on a globe, representing hope, aspiration and spirituality. It's also referred to as the *Ring of Thanksgiving*, but Belfast folk love nicknames, so it is more commonly known as *Nuala with the Hula* or the *Doll on the Ball*.

McHugh's dates back to 1711.

Queen's Square

Pass the Laganside Bus Centre and just beyond 'The Boat' apartment complex, glance left to see one of the city's most appealing vistas, **Queen's Square**. Until the 1840s, ships were tied up here at quays named after the Donegall family.

On the square stands what is Belfast's answer to Pisa's leaning tower, topped by the Gothic **Albert Memorial Clock ❼**.

The 113ft (34m) column is named after Queen Victoria's stern consort,

Waterfront art

Exploration of Lanyon Place will uncover a scattering of interesting pieces of art and sculpture. Notable are Andy Scott's *Beacon of Hope* (2007) on Thanksgiving Square; Rita Duffy's *Dreams* (2004) on the Lanyon Quay building; *Barrel Man* (1997) by Ross Wilson on Café Terrace; and *Sheep on the Road* (1991) by Deborah Brown. Visit Belfast has a good online guide to street art in Belfast, including the waterfront area (www.visitbelfast.com/article/virtual-street-art-tour).

Watch out for sheep on the Road at Lanyon Place.

Custom House.

who is displayed in his Garter robes. Lanyon secretly joined the committee that chose its design, but a decision to award him the contract was declared improper, and the work went to his rival William Barre.

Built over reclaimed land, where once boats sailed down the River Farset (which now runs underneath), it had developed such a serious list that it almost matched that of its askew Italian rival. A painstaking restoration in 2003 ensured a more solid base and a shinier facade, but stand back, look up and you can still see a slight tilt.

McHugh's ❽ (see page 67), on the left, claims to be Belfast's oldest surviving building, dating to 1711. This area once housed a raffish collection of bordello taverns (a history reflected in one or two cheeky details in the bar's interior), including Madame Du Barry's, where painter Stanley Spencer supped while his brother Gilbert 'Professor' Spencer played cathouse piano in the 1940s. Artfully restored, it is a successful mixture of old and new, with good food including Irish boxty (a traditional potato pancake) and live music.

Across the square is another of Lanyon's solid accomplishments in Portland stone, rich in Ionic and Doric columns. Built in 1852, it has been home to both the Northern Bank and the First Trust Bank.

Custom House Square

Beyond, to the north, **Custom House Square** has been restored to become, once again, the most important public space in Belfast. What had, in the nineteenth and early twentieth centuries, been the lively Belfast version of 'Speakers' Corner' is marked with a life-size bronze statue, The Speaker; the square's surrounding copper lights continue the theme with their nickname 'The Hecklers'.

The square also includes Belfast's oldest drinking fountain for horses, the Calder fountain, revived to its former glory. A water feature traces the course

Shimmering reflections along the riverside walk.

of the Farset River beneath, and there is a play area for children too.

Over the years it has witnessed everything from strongman competitions, circuses and carnivals to outdoor theatre performances, as well as Belfast's first outdoor Christmas ice rink and an annual Oktoberfest beer festival. The yearly CHSq series of concerts welcomes international pop and rock acts to the stage. It's also popular with skateboarders.

The magnificent Palladian simplicity of the **Custom House** ❾ itself is the very zenith of Lanyon's achievements. Its real delight is a pediment of Britannia, Mercury and Neptune flanked by a lion and unicorn, amid capstans and knots, executed by the great stonemason Thomas Fitzpatrick and seen best from the Lagan Weir and Lookout. The novelist Anthony Trollope (1815–82) worked in the Custom House as a post office official in the 1850s.

The Lagan

Our attention turns back to the river, which flows into Belfast Lough. The now-defunct Laganside Corporation

was set up in 1989 to reclaim, revitalise and gentrify the Lagan's banks, and it did its job well. The Lagan flows through the culture of the people of Belfast, much as it flows through the city. It is commemorated in songs such as *My Lagan Love*, sung as a traditional Irish air, and the saying: "Do you think I came up the Lagan in a bubble?" meaning, do you think I'm daft/gullible?

The scheme also maintained a satisfactory water level upstream with

Cleaning up the Lagan

Due to the massive purification measures carried out by Laganside Corporation, involving the construction of Lagan Weir, recultivating tributaries, dredging the banks and the installation of an aeration system, the River Lagan is welcoming back increasing numbers of plopping grey mullet, homing Atlantic salmon and wild brown trout to its greatly improved waters. From the Lagan Weir and Lookout, it is possible to occasionally spot seals.

Belfast's history depicted on the
Big Fish's ceramic scales.

The Salmon of Knowledge

The *Salmon of Knowledge* is a 32ft (10m) ceramic salmon, commissioned to celebrate the return of the species to the cleaned-up River Lagan. Created in 1999 by local artist John Kindness, the 'skin' is decorated with a mosaic of texts relating to Belfast's history, from material from Tudor times to recent newspaper headlines, and contributions from Belfast schoolchildren. It is nicknamed, simply, the *Big Fish*.

the construction of **Lagan Weir** (see box) which, at a cost of £14 million, was one of the largest civil engineering projects ever to be undertaken in Northern Ireland at the time. In the event of a high tide, the weir acts as a tidal barrage and can be used to protect the city from flooding.

The Corporation has also improved public access, devising, among other things, an attractive riverside walk (see Tour 6).

Today, new and refurbished buildings overlook the river, making this one of the prime property locations in Belfast.

Donegall Quay

Just downstream of the weir is the pedestrianised **Donegall Quay**, with its massive river wall, bordered on one side with jetties and slipways; on the other, by practical but ornamental stone paviours and square-setts pierced by black bollards bearing the gilt seahorse from the city's coat of arms. Near here, in a city that is distinctive for the human scale of its buildings, is Ireland's tallest habitable building, the 26-storey Obel (standing for 'an obelisk set in old Belfast').

From here, by the **Big Fish** ❿ sculpture – aka the *Salmon of Knowledge* – which celebrates the return of fish to the Lagan (see box), Waterways Belfast (www.waterwaysbelfast.com) offers a ninety-minute tour of Belfast's waterfront. The leisurely journey takes in the docks where RMS *Titanic* was built, including the RMS *Titanic* slipway, then passes HMS *Caroline*, a restored

Belfast Harbour Office clock.

The monumental 'Samson and Goliath' cranes dominate Belfast's skyline.

World War One warship, before traversing the Musgrave channel, where you can spot seals, and sailing past the iconic Harland & Wolff cranes, Samson and Goliath.

The Docks

North along Donegall Quay, past the former ferry terminal, is Corporation

The bronze sculpture, *Dividers*, at Clarendon Dock.

Square with an elegant sandstone **Harbour Office ⓫**, an Italianate building decked out by Lanyon's partner, W.H. Lynn. Its boardroom features the captain's table and chairs that were destined for the RMS *Titanic* but completed too late for the voyage, and is rich in fine historical paintings, including one of Captain Pirrie, grandfather to William, whose expansionist vision gave birth to the doomed liner.

Just to the west of this is the late-1850s Italianate **Sinclair Seamen's Presbyterian Church ⓬**, designed by Lanyon. Its interior owes more,

The Belfast Barge

Moored at Lanyon Quay on the River Lagan, the Belfast Barge (www.belfastbarge.org) is Northern Ireland's only floating arts centre. Owned by the not-for-profit charity Lagan Legacy, it hosts live music, a cinema club and family days featuring baby raves. It also houses a maritime museum, telling the industrial history of Belfast, once the world's biggest shipbuilding city.

The stylish *Malmaison* hotel, a converted seed warehouse.

however, to an optimist and imbiber, the Reverend Sam Cochrane RN. The pitch-pine pulpit takes the shape of a ship's prow flanked by navigation lights. The font is a ship's binnacle. The bell of HMS *Hood* calls lost souls to service and collection boxes take the form of lifeboats. By the door a text reads: 'A Merry Heart Doeth Good Like a Medicine'.

It is still the traditional duty of each incumbent minister to visit every ship that docks in Belfast Harbour. The church is open to the public most

Sailortown

North of Clarendon Dock was a once-thriving dockland community known as Sailortown, and since 2009 it has undergone redevelopment. New housing has changed the character of the area, but it retains a whiff of its old atmosphere. To experience a true Belfast caff, stop off at the 1972-born *Benny's Café* on Short Street (tel: 028-9074 3128) and tuck into the signature Benny's Belfast Bap.

Wednesday afternoons, 2–4.30pm, and is well worth a visit.

Clarendon Dock

North of the Harbour Office, Clarendon Road leads into the redeveloped and attractive tree-lined riverside plazas surrounding **Clarendon Dock** ⑬. The trees are ash and oak, the boulevards laid with stone paviours and square-setts, like those on Donegall Quay, and many of the laid-up anchors and half-buried cannon bollards are authentic. Unable to pass unnoticed, the Vivien Burnside bronze sculpture, *Dividers*, represents an archway, as the viewer looks inwards to the changing city or outwards to the sea.

Across the River Lagan looms the huge yellow upturned 'U's of the Samson and Goliath cranes, and the SSE Arena (see Tour 9).

Victoria Street

Turning back, through Clarendon Dock and then west along Corporation Square and under the motorway, we eventually join Victoria Street and continue until we reach High Street. While the Chapel of the Ford stood on the corner of High Street from at least 1306, its ultimate successor, the high Anglican **St George's**, dates only from 1813. Its classical portico was brought from the Earl Bishop of Derry's unfinished house. Perks for its first choir boys included all the salmon they could catch from the River Farset beyond the original wrought-iron rear gates. A simple memorial to Henry Pottinger is in tune with its plain interior.

Carry on along Victoria Street to the **Malmaison hotel** ⑭ (see page 125) with its curious frontage. The building is decorated with Thomas Fitzpatrick's splendid stonework, first devised for Lytle's and McCausland's

Victoria Square glass-domed viewing gallery.

Warehouses (rival seed merchants), at Nos. 34–8 Victoria Street. For Lytle he carved frogs between water lilies, squirrels eating nuts, plus an assortment of exotic birds. For McCausland he represented the five trading continents in five robustly non-PC heads: Africa – an Ethiopian slave with broken chain and Nile lily; Asia – a Chinese girl in silks; Oceania – a South Sea Islander with coconuts; Europe – a be-whiskered and self-satisfied Caucasian; North America – a Native American complete with tomahawk and feather headdress.

Bittles Bar (see page 67), probably the world's only triangular pub, is tucked into the flatiron-shaped building at the corner of Victoria Street and Upper Church Lane. This watering hole was once known as the *Shakespeare* and was patronised by performers from nearby theatres.

Victoria Square

Just across the street, the venerable **Kitchen Bar** (see page 67) has settled in well to its new digs, having had to move out of its nearby 1859-built premises due to the construction of the mammoth **Victoria Square** ⑮ in 2008. This four-floor shopping, dining and leisure complex is topped by a massive glass dome and viewing gallery, from which you can gain a good grasp of the dimensions of the cityscape and surrounding hills. Standing at the entrance is the eye-catching Victorian **Jaffe Fountain**, made in 1874 by George Smith & Company in Glasgow. It is dedicated to Daniel Joseph Jaffe (1809–74) who was born in Mecklenburg, Germany, and was responsible for laying the foundation stone of the synagogue in Great Victoria Street. Jaffe is buried in the Jewish plot at Belfast Cemetery. His son, Otto, was elected as Belfast's first lord mayor in 1899, knighted after his first term, and re-elected in 1904.

Chichester Street

Back on Victoria Street once more, carry on and then take the first right into Chichester (which local people pronounce Chai-Chester) Street; look eastwards for a splendid vista of the imposing Lanyon Place, then west to the Black Mountain. The pleasant *Garrick Bar* at No. 29, built in 1810, took its name from the famous English actor; its current customers ply other stages – although they may be just as dramatic – the nearby Petty Sessions and Royal Courts of Justice.

Just to the west, Nos. 7–11 form an excellently restored terrace of four-storey Georgian houses built in dusky brick and dating from 1804. They

almost complete this route, which now proceeds across Donegall Square East from the red sandstone of the Ocean Buildings, rich in elaborate carvings of mermaids and monsters.

To finish as we started, right in the corner of the City Hall grounds, there stands – with ship's plans in hand – yet another reminder of the RMS *Titanic*: a Sicilian marble statue of Sir Edward James Harland of Harland & Wolff.

Eating out

Bittles Bar
70 Upper Church Lane; www.bittlesbar.com.
Housed in a flatiron-shaped building, this is one of the city's more unusual pubs. Inside, bright murals depict the Troubles and gilded shamrocks bring the tavern to life. Popular with shoppers who drop by for refreshments at reasonable prices. ££

Galley Café
Titanic Belfast, 1 Olympic Way, Queen's Road; www.titanicbelfast.com.
On the ground floor of the Titanic Belfast attraction, you can grab a table for a warming bowl of soup or pick up sandwich or sweet pastry to go. It's a handy place to rest after an RMS *Titanic* tour, and is close to the gift shop. £

The Kitchen Bar
1 Victoria Square; www.thekitchenbar.com.
Relocated from its original site around the corner to accommodate the Victoria Square development, nothing else has changed at *The Kitchen Bar* – it's still friendly and renowned for its quality, home-cooked traditional food. The Irish pub classics on the menu are particularly hearty, though there are lighter bites too. ££

Malmaison Bar & Grill
34–38 Victoria Street; www.malmaison.com/locations/belfast/bar-grill.
Elegant booths and comfy chairs provide the perfect blend of sumptuous surroundings and an informal atmosphere. The menu of locally sourced food lets you sample uncomplicated fusion-style cuisine. Afternoon tea is popular, and there's a great selection of cocktails. £££

McHugh's
29–31 Queen's Square; www.mchughsbar.com.
A traditional drinking den retaining many of its original features, dating from 1711. Expect local pub classics such as boxty and baked gammon, as well as 'hot rock' steaks cooked at your table on a volcanic rock. A kids' menu is available. ££

OX
1 Oxford Street; www.oxbelfast.com.
Housed in an old building opposite the river, the pared-down minimalist interior reflects the modern approach to the menu in this Michelin-starred restaurant. Ingredients are sourced locally and carefully chosen before making their way onto the plate. The set-course tasting menus mirror the changing seasons. £££

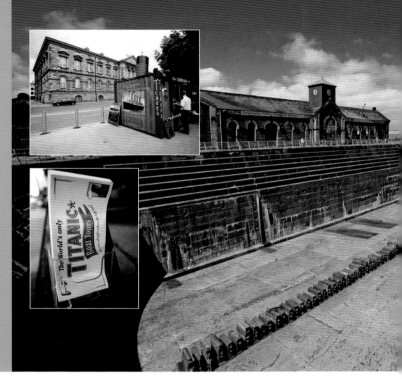

RMS TITANIC

The design and construction of RMS *Titanic* played a huge part in Belfast's shipbuilding heritage but the events that followed cemented the city's place in history forever.

Despite its tragic watery fate in 1912, RMS *Titanic* was a remarkable feat of Edwardian engineering – innovative, superbly crafted and built on an extraordinary scale. It was, in other words, an appropriate and easily identifiable symbol of Belfast's pre-eminence as a shipbuilder. By the time City Hall was completed in 1906, the city was not only one of the world's greatest ports but also a world leader in ropemaking, tobacco, linen and other industries. RMS *Titanic* was thus built at the apex of Belfast's ambition, belief and sense of self-importance. Designed and built in the city between 1909 and 1912 and waved off on her maiden voyage on 2 April 1912, she was the most luxuriously appointed ship ever seen – and the pride and joy of shipbuilders Harland & Wolff.

The Titanic boom

More than one hundred years on, few now question the wisdom of Belfast identifying itself with a ship famous

RMS *Titanic*'s dry dock and pumphouse.

Tours

Throughout the streets of Belfast there are numerous buildings and monuments with links to RMS *Titanic*. A myriad of guided tours provides an insight into the remarkable history of Belfast's greatest attraction. The best starting point for a self-guided tour is the Titanic Belfast visitor centre. For more information about RMS *Titanic* visit the website of the Belfast Titanic Society at www.belfast-titanic.com.

FEATURE TOURS

RMS Titanic in numbers

It cost **$7,500,000** to build RMS *Titanic*.
The launch took **62** seconds to complete.
There were **29** boilers on board and her forward anchor weighed nearly **16** tons.
More than **3 million** rivets were used in the building of the ship.
She was **882ft** (**268m**) long and weighed **46,328 tons** fully loaded.
She had **5 miles** (**8km**) of decks, squash courts, and was the first vessel to have a heated swimming pool.
First-class passengers paid a whopping **$4350** for a parlour suite ticket.
RMS *Titanic* hit an iceberg on Sunday 14 April 1912 at about **11.40pm** and sank at **2.20am** on 15 April.
The ship was loaded with only enough lifeboats for **1178** people; there were **2228** people on board.
The largest percentage of survivors were first-class passengers.
The *Titanic* lies **12,460ft** (**3798m**) down at the bottom of the Atlantic.
Of the **1517** people who perished, only **337** bodies were recovered.

for sinking on its maiden voyage. As a popular tourist t-shirt says: 'she was alright when she left here'. This city is very proud of its associations with the greatest liner ever. For the centennial commemorations in 2012, it unveiled the spectacular Titanic Belfast visitor centre, with a multi-million-pound refreshment following in 2023, while the Belfast Maritime Festival is a major event on the city's cultural calendar of happenings. The Titanic Quarter, a £1-billion mini-city of apartments, hotels, restaurants, bars and visitor attractions spread across 185 acres (75 hectares) of the former shipyard and birthplace of the legendary liner, is dedicated to this amazing ship (see page 84), as is the Titanic Quarter campus of Belfast Metropolitan College.

Lagan Meadows.

TOUR 6
Riverside walk

A circular stroll of 3.5 miles (5.5km), along the banks
of the River Lagan from the centre of Belfast, with
the option of a longer towpath bike ride.

This tour follows the waterside walkway
both sides of the riverbank, pausing
in Ormeau Park. Alternatively, you
can hire a bike and explore the Lagan
Towpath, a total of 11 miles (18km),
taking you all the way to Lisburn.

Starting the walk

Starting at **Waterfront Hall ❶** the
river pathway heads south along the
left bank to May's Meadow, where it
crosses Albert Bridge to St George's
Harbour and continues past the
business park. Continue to **Ormeau
Bridge**; cross the bridge and take the
first gates into **Ormeau Park ❷** (free),
which features some unusual trees,
eco-trails and orienteering courses,
and has a children's playground and
bowling greens.

> ## Highlights
> • Waterfront Hall
> • Ormeau Park
> • Cycling the Lagan Towpath
> • Lagan Meadows
> • Barnett's Demesne

The bridges

Leave the park on the east side onto
Ravenhill Road and continue to
Albert Bridge. Cross the road and
rejoin the towpath, continuing to
Laganview, Gregg's Quay and under
Queen's Bridge. At the next bridge,
Queen Elizabeth II Bridge, go under
the main road, pick up the path again
and continue to **Lagan Weir**, a good
place to cross back to the west bank.

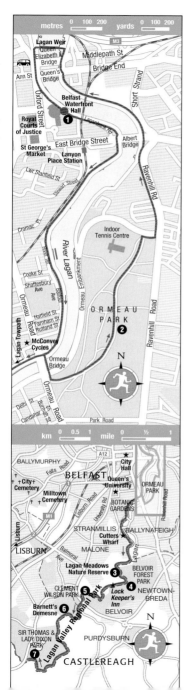

Cycling the towpath

To hire a bike, consider signing up for the **Belfast Bike** scheme (www. belfastbikes.co.uk), with fifty docking stations dotted across the city. The first half hour is free; the charge is then £1 per hour for the next four hours and £2 per half-hour afterwards.

Along the canal, linen barons' mansions recall its role in a nineteenth-century plan to create a Belfast-to-Dublin water route. The path dips through grasslands into **Lagan Meadows Nature Reserve** ❸. Another footbridge across the Lagan cuts into **Belvoir Forest Park** ❹. Otherwise, follow the left bank downstream, crossing a wooded island between canal and river. Left-bank explorers can continue upstream by **Clement Wilson Park** ❺, and past **Shaw's Bridge**, where there's a possible diversion to **Barnett's Demesne** ❻ with an elegant 1820s house, restaurant and art gallery. Another point of interest is **Sir Thomas and Lady Dixon Park** ❼ with its mansion and magnificent rolling acres. The towpath wiggles on to Lisburn.

Eating out

Cutters Wharf
Lockview Road, Stranmillis; www.cutterswharf.co.uk.
A bistro-style menu filled with reinterpreted classics and modern flavours, alongside daily specials. Dine outside on the spacious terrace, overlooking the river, in fine weather. ££

The Lock Keeper's Inn
2 Lock Keeper's Lane, Lagan towpath; tel: 028-9064 0088.
Snacks, ranging from sandwiches to scones, sausage rolls and soups, are served at this idyllic location overlooking the River Lagan. £

Clifton House.

TOUR 7
Northern suburbs

This 7-mile (11km) drive incorporates one of Belfast's most infamous stretches of road; afterwards, visit Belfast Castle then take the challenge of a 2-mile (4km) uphill walk.

Close to the city centre along the once troublesome Crumlin Road and in the Ardoyne district are some grim reminders of a turbulent past. It is hard to believe that the pleasant suburbs and Belfast Hills are so close at hand, where you can discover riches such as Belfast Castle and the zoo, and throw caution to the wind and climb high above the city. If you don't want to drive, take the direct route to the castle or the zoo on Metro bus 1 from the city centre, heading out along the Antrim Road.

Clifton Street

From the city centre strike out along Donegall Street, which leads into Clifton Street, and the junction of North Queen Street. Opened in

Highlights
- Clifton House
- Crumlin Road Gaol
- Belfast Castle
- Cave Hill
- Belfast Zoo

1774 and Belfast's original Poor House, **Clifton House** ❶ (2 North Queen Street; www.cliftonbelfast. com), though much altered, is still one of the most delightfully modest public Georgian buildings in the city, and one of Belfast's oldest. After lengthy restoration works, the building is now a unique cultural space and event venue and a Heritage Centre which runs guided

Statue of King William III on top of Belfast Orange Hall on Clifton Street.

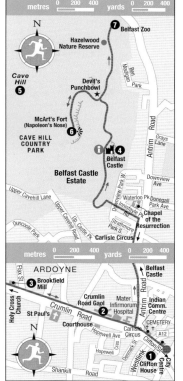

walking, graveyard and house tours on Fridays and Saturdays.

Opposite, at 86 Clifton Street, is the **Indian Community Centre** (www.iccbelfast.org) housing a Hindu temple. It organises many events throughout the year, including the well-attended Mela festival each August, which brings thousands to the Botanic Gardens for Indian dancing, music, fashion and food.

One of the most important burial sites in Belfast is the **Clifton Street Cemetery**, where a great number of pioneers of Belfast life lie, including politicians, journalists, Henry Joy McCracken and his sister Mary Ann, and the man who coined the phrase 'Emerald Isle', Dr William Drennan.

Crumlin Road Gaol

North past Carlisle Circus are Charles Lanyon's deliberately sinister **Crumlin Road Gaol** ❷ (www.crumlinroadgaol. com) and his formidable Corinthian **Courthouse** (now derelict and fire damaged), squaring up to one another across Crumlin Road (and joined by a tunnel below). During the worst years of the Troubles, between 1969 and 1996, the prison held some of the most notorious murderers, including many involved in paramilitary violence. After closing in 1996 it

reopened as a tourist attraction in 2012, transformed to reflect the way it looked in Victorian times. A ninety-minute tour takes in the holding, punishment and condemned cells. Having shaken off its grim past, it now hosts family fun events, live music, ghost tours and even weddings. McConnell's Distillery and Visitor Experience is scheduled to open in the building in 2024.

Further on up Crumlin Road is the beautifully converted **Brookfield Mill** ❸, once part of Belfast's linen industry and now providing homes and office space. At the apex of Crumlin Road and nearby Woodvale, the Peace Line marks off Catholic Ardoyne, where

Saving Cave Hill

The Cave Hill Conservation Campaign (www.cavehillconservation.org) is a voluntary organisation originally founded in 1989 to stop the prospecting of minerals taking place in this place of outstanding natural beauty. Its remit has extended beyond this, and the group is dedicated to preserving Cave Hill by reducing litter, planting trees and keeping rights of way open, as well as organising wildlife events and collecting data. The area is well worth preserving; on a clear day you can see the hills of the Lake District on the UK mainland.

some 20,000 people were employed in the linen mills. Look out for Ross Wilson's bronze statute, *The Mill Worker*, outside the building, inspired by the artist William Conor's depiction of the 'shawlies' (female mill workers, or 'millies').

Belfast Hills

Returning to Carlisle Circus, turn north into the lengthy **Antrim Road**, and you will pass the pleasant Waterworks Park, which dates from an 1840s attempt to solve Belfast's growing water needs.

Looking west, north or east from almost anywhere in Belfast you can see how the city is cradled in the belly of a geographical basin, surrounded by hills. Clockwise from the west, these are Black Mountain, Cave Hill, the Castlereagh Hills and the drumlins of County Down, all framed at the ends of the shallow canyons of the streets.

Just over 1.5 miles (2km) on along Antrim Road is Innisfayle Park Road, which leads to Belfast Castle.

Belfast Castle

Follow the road into the castle estate and up to **Belfast Castle** ❹ (www.belfastcastle.co.uk; free), a ruggedly romantic Scots baronial pile rich in turrets and faced with Cookstown sandstone. It was built in 1865 for the impoverished third marquis of Donegall, by Charles Lanyon's son, John, who borrowed freely from Prince Albert's sketches for Balmoral Castle. John Lanyon's fees were guaranteed by the marquis's daughter, Harriet, who had taken the sensible precaution of marrying the immensely rich eighth earl of Shaftesbury. Their son, the ninth earl, presented the castle to the city in 1934. Private tours of the castle are available on request. There is also the *Cellar* restaurant and an excellent adventure

The breathtaking view from Cave Hill.

The grounds of Belfast Castle with a cat mosaic.

playground in the grounds. The drive continues back to the Antrim Road north towards Belfast Zoo.

The Cave Hill Visitor Centre at the castle has detailed walking maps and other information on the building's history as well as its natural surroundings in the Cave Hill Country Park.

Cave Hill Walk

We now begin our **Cave Hill ❺** walk proper through the 200-acre (80-hectare) estate. Take the Cave Hill Trail from the car park. From the woods a steeper path climbs all the way to the **Devil's Punchbowl**, first used by Neolithic hunter-gatherers. Just before this cave the trail swerves left and runs steeply towards a defensive ditch to **McArt's Fort ❻** on the 1180ft (360m) -high promontory. This is alternatively referred to as **Napoleon's Nose** or Ben Madigan (from *beann*, the Irish for peak) after a ninth-century king of Ulster. The outline of Cave Hill has been likened to an outline of Napoleon sleeping on the hillside, the fort representing his nose. Here, foxes trail rabbits through the heather and badgers wander at night through the bluebells in May.

Belfast Zoo

The Cave Trail continues to Hightown Fort, but if you wish to walk to the zoo, return part way to the Devil's Punchbowl and take the path north, along to **Hazelwood Nature Reserve**. This path brings you to the fringes of **Belfast Zoo ❼** (www.belfastcity.gov.uk/zoo/home).

Opened in 1934 at the end of a tram route, as part of a pleasure ground called Bellevue Gardens, the zoo has a pleasantly old-fashioned feel, but, in fact, is remarkably progressive in its captive breeding programme for rare animals. The views from here are particularly splendid. Lemurs stroll freely around the zoo; the African enclosure and the penguin and sea-lion pools are popular with children. The Adventurers' Learning Centre is the zoo's play area. The website offers information on its 'Keeper for a Day' and 'Meet the Animals' programmes.

Eating out

Castle Tavern
Belfast Castle, Antrim Road; www.belfastcastle.co.uk.
A handy place to grab a bite, *Castle Tavern* serves up Ulster frys, sausage baps and pancakes, as well as soups, sandwiches, kids' meals and snacks. It is run by the *Ability Café*, which provides meaningful employment for people with a disability or health condition. £

Treetop Tearooms
Belfast Zoo, Antrim Road; www.belfastcity.gov.uk/zoo/home.
This is a takeaway-only café providing hot and cold light snacks and ice cream, but it affords a spectacular view over Belfast Lough and the zoo. Near the zoo's entrance, the *Zoo Café* has indoor and outdoor seating and serves hot meals. £

Mural in Falls Road commemorating Bobby Sands.

TOUR 8
West Belfast

This 2.5-mile (4km) half-day walk covers one of the most absorbing and controversial Belfast districts, now becoming the focus of a tourist boom.

West Belfast has witnessed some unthinkable things in its turbulent past and this tour gives the opportunity to learn and understand what life was like before, after and during the Troubles. Many famous landmarks from over three decades of the area's history are here. One of the most striking discoveries is just how closely situated the Shankill and Falls roads are, where two very different communities still live. The tour follows the length of both roads and enables you to cross the Peace Line.

Taking a taxi

As an alternative to this walk, you might consider taking one of the famous **Black Taxi Tours** (try Big E's Belfast Taxi Tours; www.big-e-

Highlights

- Murals
- Clonard Monastery
- An Cultúrlann McAdam Ó Fiaich
- City Cemetery
- Peace Line
- St Matthew's Church

taxitours.com or Belfast Black Cab Tours; www.belfastblackcabtours.co.uk). They give a detailed insight into the area, its people and what makes the district what it is today.

Falls Road

For republican west Belfast, start at the city centre end (take Metro bus 10) of **Falls Road**, at the junction with Northumberland Street. Though many high-rise tower blocks have been demolished, the Divis Tower, to the east, is still standing as a testament to the horrors of the Troubles. The British army set up an observation point on the top two floors, which could only be accessed by helicopter. This is where nine-year-old Patrick Rooney – the first child victim of the Troubles – was killed in 1969. Just off Falls Road is **St Peter's Cathedral** ❶ (St Peter's Square; tel: 028-9032 7573), whose two great towers with rising spires were used as sightlines by German bombers in World War II.

Conway Mill ❷ (5–7 Conway Street; www.conway-mill.ie), on the second turning to the right up Falls Road, was built in 1842 by the Kennedy family, and it was the first flax-spinning mill in west Belfast. A listed building, it ceased production in 1972 and is now a centre for more than twenty local craftspeople, including artists and jewellery-makers.

It also houses the small **Irish Republican History Museum**, which is entirely run by volunteers and displays a fascinating range of exhibits and artefacts.

Bobby Sands Memorial
Back on Falls Road, just two streets up on the right at 49 Falls Road, is the iconic memorial mural for Bobby Sands. A member of the Provisional IRA, Sands was elected MP when on hunger strike in prison, where he was held for his part in helping to plan a 1976 bombing. In May 1981 he was the first of the ten republican hunger strikers to die, aged 27, after 66 days without food.

Clonard Monastery
A little further on, at the end of Clonard Street, is **Clonard Monastery** ❸ (www.clonard.com). Built in French Gothic style with a striking 20ft (6m) -wide stained-glass rose window, the impressive church and monastery were completed in 1911. Floor and ceiling mosaics trace the history of its owners, the Redemptorist order, a Catholic movement founded in Italy in 1732. In early summer, the church hosts a nine-day Novena when the grounds are crowded with the faithful. It is here that vital talks were held that ultimately led to the peace process. The church is also used as part

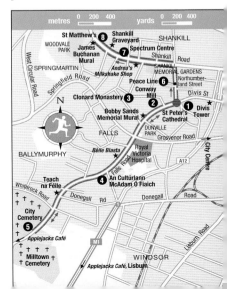

of the Féile an Phobail, aka the West Belfast Festival (see page 79), and hosts concerts and events.

On the other side of Falls Road, Dunville Park is named after its whiskey-distilling benefactor, who donated the green space to the people of the city in 1887. Located within its parameters is the famous Dunville Fountain, which has been refurbished and is now filled with thousands of flowers. Further up the road, the sprawling grounds of Royal Victoria Hospital still house the world's first air-conditioning ducts. Another regular venue for the Féile an Phobail is St Mary's University College to the right, designed in High Victorian style and dating from 1900.

Gaeltacht Quarter

This district is focused on Falls Road. Continuing along the road

Clonard Monastery.

and central to this area is **An Cultúrlann McAdam Ó Fiaich** ❹ (www.culturlann.ie), a three-storey Irish language, arts and cultural centre at No. 216, in a former Presbyterian Church. It has a café, Irish-language book and gift shop, theatre and tourist information point. On the ground floor, the Dillon Gallery, named after the Falls Road artist Gerard Dillon, mounts exhibits by local and international artists.

The building also hosts summer schools, Irish-language classes, traditional and contemporary music sessions, concerts, lectures and events for children. A thirtieth anniversary project in 2021 researched the importance of the heritage and history associated with An Chultúrlann. Pause for a coffee and discover the essence of west Belfast culture.

From here you can book political walking tours of the area, organised by former republican prisoners. Coiste (St Comgall's, Divis Street; www.coiste. ie) runs tours that gather at Divis Tower in the Lower Falls and visits the murals of Falls Road. It can be arranged to hand you over to former loyalist prisoners at the Peace Line for a tour of the Shankill Road. There are also tours focusing on the Milltown Cemetery, the Ballymurphy housing estate and the history of the United Irishmen. Tours are available in several European languages. Tickets can be purchased at the Belfast Welcome Centre (www.visitbelfast.com) or through the Coiste website; booking is essential.

Féile an Phobail

Féile An Phobail (www.feilebelfast. com), also known as the West Belfast Festival, or simply Féile, is an annual summer celebration held every August. The organisers' office is just up the road at Nos. 141–43 Falls Road. The

Celtic cross headstones at Milltown Cemetery.

original event has spawned several others over subsequent years, including the Draíocht Children's Arts festival and the annual Spring Festival (Féile An Earraigh) in March. Its name translates as 'community festival' and it draws in people from across the city and beyond with its mixture of music, drama, literary events and comedy, starring local and international big names such as Roddy Doyle, Westlife and the Harlem Gospel Choir. Highlights include political debates and a colourful parade up the Falls. It is now the biggest community-based festival in Ireland.

The cemeteries

Pushing on to the top end of Falls Road you reach the cemeteries. Though it might seem perverse, one of the most fascinating tours in Belfast is during the festival when a local Sinn Féin councillor and former Belfast Lord Mayor, Tom Hartley, takes visitors on a ninety-minute journey around the **City Cemetery** ❺ and **Milltown Cemetery**, the former owned by Belfast City Council, the latter by the Catholic Church. Milltown, where, in 1988 and on live TV, loyalist paramilitary Michael Stone shot and threw grenades at mourners attending a republican funeral, includes the plot where hunger striker Bobby Sands is buried.

A sunken wall prevents Catholic and Protestant bodies from mingling underground in the City Cemetery, opened in 1869. One of the oldest cemeteries in Belfast, many prominent citizens of Victorian society are laid to rest here. A new visitor centre opened

Founding the Féile

Féile An Phobail (West Belfast Festival) was founded in 1988 when the Falls Road district was described by the international media as a broken, crime-ridden community. The founders were determined to promote the positive side of the neighbourhood and the event has gone from strength to strength, creating one of the best-attended festivals in the city, bringing in some 50,000 people. It's a great time to be in town.

Painted walls on Shankill Road.

in 2023, as part of the City Cemetery Heritage Project, and features an interpretative exhibition, interactive features for children, and workstations for curious people carrying out genealogy research into the 220,000-plus people buried here. Visitors can download a free app and take self-guided tours.

Our tour now circles back down Falls Road; you may choose to

Shankill street art

Lack of resources have often blighted the Shankill, a heartland of working-class loyalism, but ongoing street art and community initiatives breathe vibrancy into the area. In 2023, a new mural of a young drummer boy was unveiled at the gateway to Shankill Road, near Peters Hill, painted by Belfast DJ-turned-street artist Glen Molloy. At Conor's Corner, named after the famed Shankill-born artist William Conor (1881–1968), a large mural, *Hope* from Dan Kitchener, features an Asian woman in vivid colours, in tribute to some of the area's newer residents.

walk, but we suggest taking either Metro bus 10 or buses 82/82A and disembarking at the corner with Northumberland Street.

Peace Line

Walk along Northumberland Street to the north and through the **Peace Line** ➏ towards **Shankill Road**. On 9 September 1969, James Chichester-Clarke, prime minister of Northern Ireland's parliament, announced that the British army would build a temporary 'peace line' between Protestant and Catholic areas of Belfast to stop rioting. By the end of the century, there were fifteen walls separating the two communities, some of them corrugated-iron barriers crowned with razor wire, others 20ft (6m) concrete barricades reminiscent of the Berlin Wall.

The most obtrusive stretched for two miles (3km), separating the Falls and Shankill roads. The walls, covered in art murals and folk graffiti, are now a tourist attraction, but some local people believe they are still in fact needed. Stormont committed to removing the peace walls by 2023 but still they stand.

Shankill Road

At the junction with Shankill Road, by the *Rex Bar*, glance across the road to the corner of Argyle Street to see a mural of Edward Carson signing the 1912 Covenant, alongside a large rendition of King Charles, unveiled to mark his coronation. Walk west and you will come to the Shankill Memorial Gardens, on the other side of the road. The gardens recall those who died in the two World Wars, with an old Belfast streetlamp lit by an 'eternal flame' commemorating the victims of the IRA's 1993 Shankill Road bombing, which killed ten people including two children.

Spectrum Centre

The **Spectrum Centre ❼** (331–33 Shankill Road; www.spectrumcentre. com) opened in 2001, a rough equivalent of An Cultúrlann McAdam Ó Fiaich on the Falls. It has become a base for community groups as well as dance, drama and music studios, sports clubs and a film society (as befits its location on the site of an old cinema).

Although unprepossessing from the outside, inside, the main auditorium hosts everything from music concerts and craft fairs to children's activities and conferences.

Churches and cemeteries

Towards the top of the road, on the right, is the Shankill Graveyard, the main city cemetery until 1866. It is said burials have taken place on this site for over 1000 years. It contains the graves of several notable citizens as well as many who died in various plagues. A statue of Queen Victoria stands by the main entrance. The name Shankill comes from the Gaelic for 'old church', the site of which, believed to date from the sixth century, can be found within the graveyard. Across the road is the Battle of the Somme Memorial Garden of Reflection, at No. 417, commemorating those who died in World War I fighting with the 36th Ulster Division.

A few steps up the road is the distinctive 1872 Church of Ireland **St Matthew's ❽**, known as the 'Shamrock Church', for its tri-cornered shape. Its holy water font is believed to be the only remnant in Belfast of the original Old Church (and whose water is also believed to be a cure for warts).

Other murals in the area feature former lord mayors, famous sons and fallen paramilitary combatants of the Troubles. Once you have finished you can catch the Metro bus 11 back to the city centre.

Eating out

Andrea's Milkshake Shop
272 Shankill Road; tel: 028-9032 9624.
If you are looking for a milkshake, slushie, ice cream or sweet treat, this is the place to come. £

Applejacks Coffee Shop
1 Caffrey Hill, Glen Road;
tel: 028-9043 1125.
Enjoy great views from the outdoor terrace of this pretty family-run café, atop Caffrey Hill. The all-day fry is

a popular choice, as are the deluxe sandwiches and the belt-loosening potato-bread stack (three potato bread, two sausages, two bacon, one egg). £

Béile Blasta
147 Falls Road; tel: 028-9032 9406.
In the heart of the Gaeltacht Quarter, this friendly restaurant serves simple, hearty food. Burgers, lasagne, soup or a curry will fill a hungry belly at a reasonable price. £

MURAL ART

From harsh political propaganda and monumental historic events to footballing and literary legends, murals on the walls of Northern Ireland's cities tell a fascinating story.

Around two thousand murals have been documented in Northern Ireland since the 1970s. The sectarian divide between Protestant and Catholic has long been an artistic preoccupation across the North. A century after Protestant William of Orange defeated his Catholic father-in-law James II at the 1690 Battle of the Boyne, artisan coach painters celebrated with gable-end paintings of 'King Billy' riding triumphant on his white horse. The first mural to appear in Belfast was in 1908, again recording William's victory at the Boyne. When partition in 1920 hived off Northern Ireland, triumphalist Orange murals were encouraged, deflecting the attention of poor Protestants from chronic unemployment and miserable housing.

A changing message

Until the 1981 IRA hunger strike, nationalists and republicans confined their icons to inside political and sporting clubs. Then, with a growing

A cross-community mural on Newtownards Road.

hark back to the B-Specials (an auxiliary police force disbanded in 1969) and to Cúchulainn, Hound of Ulster, and leader of the 100 BC Red Branch Knights.

Meanwhile, in Catholic north and west Belfast, the icons became the lily of the 1916 Easter Rising, Cúchulainn (the republican version), dead hunger strikers and expressions of solidarity with Mexican and Basque revolutionaries. Some read *'saoirse'* (freedom); others, in the past, displayed a morbid humour in such altered traffic signs as 'sniper at work'.

Another noted collection of murals is in the Bogside area of Derry City. Most famous is the 'Free Derry' mural declaring the area's 'independence' from British rule (see page 95).

The twenty-first century

Travel along Belfast's Falls and Shankill roads and you will see some of the most poignant tributes to those who died during the Troubles. Faces of the young look down on passing tourists, a haunting reminder of those harrowing years. The mural of IRA hunger striker Bobby Sands (see page 77), unveiled in Falls Road in 2000, is one of the most visited in the city. But the peace process has brought new hope to the city and the Falls and Shankill communities are rebuilding their lives.

Murals have evolved as a peaceful, yet powerful, art form, such as the images in East Belfast (see page 86) to C.S. Lewis and George Best, and tributes to one of the most poignant of Belfast icons, the RMS *Titanic*. Artwork supporting the Palestinian cause have started to appear in republican west Belfast. Belfast's murals are attracting a new generation of tourists but remain a compelling reminder of the past and a persuasive tool for the future.

confidence that they would triumph over Protestants as Protestants had over them, republican murals were born. Protestant murals, on the other hand, had been restricted to references to 1914 gun running, portraits of English royals, biblical prophecies and portraits of William. Now, Protestant paramilitaries saw their role as defenders of the faith. Contemporary military hardware appeared, and the murals became increasingly aggressive in nature. The images underlined the importance of the communities, where the borders lay and whose turf it was.

Sectarian murals

Along Sandy Row, the Shankill and Newtownards roads, predominantly working-class Protestant heartlands, are loyalist organisation murals which

The aluminium exterior of Titanic Belfast.

TOUR 9

Titanic Quarter and eastern suburbs

From Queen's Island to the home of the Northern Ireland Assembly, this half-day, 10-mile (16km) east Belfast drive reveals many fascinating sights.

The eastern edges of the city have grown up around its shipyard, Harland & Wolff, where a large number of east Belfast's population once worked. Now shipbuilding is overshadowed by the Titanic Quarter. This huge, disparate section, with suburbs, parks and estates, covers a large area from the leafy to the gritty, but there is much to see, from the Titanic Belfast attraction to the origins of an unlikely duo of famous sons, C. S. Lewis and George Best.

Titanic Quarter

The natural starting point for a tour of the Titanic Quarter is **Titanic Belfast** ❶ on Queen's Road (www.titanic belfast.com), which opened in 2012 to commemorate the 100th anniversary of the liner's sinking. A £4.5m revamp

Highlights

- Titanic Belfast Visitor Centre
- Titanic's Dock and Pumphouse
- SS Nomadic
- Samson and Goliath
- The Odyssey
- Landmarks of east Belfast's famous sons
- Parliament Buildings and Stormont castle grounds

and a 2023 relaunch saw the inclusion of some rare artefacts from the stricken vessel. The venue has quickly established itself as a world-class attraction. The building's startling six-storey, bow-shaped, aluminium facade reflects the lines of the ship. Inside,

Finding your way

It's fair to say that the Glider, the name of Translink's rapid transit system, transformed public transport between Belfast's west and east, via Titanic Quarter, when it was introduced in 2018. For those who want to sightsee by bus, check out the cross-city Glider Experience map available to download (www.visiteastside.com/listing/glider-experience; free). It features the main sights on the different G1 and G2 lines, so load up your DayLink smartcard and get going. A north–south city route has now been confirmed, to launch in 2027.

It operated as a shuttle ship delivering 142 first-class passengers to RMS *Titanic* in Cherbourg before she set sail across the Atlantic. Interpretative galleries and displays bring alive what it was like for the workers and passengers. The ship is berthed at the Hamilton Graving Dock and admission is included with the Titanic Experience ticket from Titanic Belfast.

Samson and Goliath

The two massive yellow gantry cranes, named after the biblical figures **Samson and Goliath**, dominate the eastern skyline over the Harland & Wolff shipyard at Queen's Island. Today the main work of the yard is in ship repair and design, but the cranes live also as a symbol of Belfast itself, featuring on T-shirts, coffee mugs and art prints.

SSE Arena

Round the corner, on Queen's Quay, the **SSE Arena** ❹ (www.ssearena belfast.com) is a large concert centre (formerly The Odyssey) welcoming international performers and home to the Belfast Giants professional ice hockey team. Also in this massive entertainment complex is a fantastic

nine galleries trace the liner's dramatic story as well as the wider theme of Belfast's seafaring and maritime heritage. To the rear are the slipways where the RMS *Titanic* was built, complete with a life-size plan of its promenade and a memorial garden.

Titanic's Dry Dock and Pumphouse

Further along Queen's Road is the 850ft (259m) -long **Thompson Dry Dock**, where the liner was built, and its adjacent **Pumphouse** ❷. Since 2023 the Pumphouse has been home to Belfast's first working distillery in ninety years, **Titanic Distillers** (www.titanic distillers.com) offering whiskey and vodka tastings, distillery and dry dock tours, and an outdoor café. Its triple-distilled single malt is a smooth, well-balanced delight. Across from the Pumphouse is HMS *Caroline*, a restored World War I ship (www.nmrn.org.uk).

SS Nomadic

Beside Titanic Belfast is the **SS Nomadic** ❸ (www.titanicbelfast. com), tender ship to RMS *Titanic* – known as her 'little sister' – and the last White Star Line ship in existence.

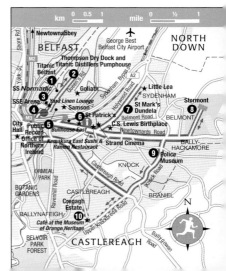

A painted tribute to C.S. Lewis.

way to keep the kids amused, the **W5** interactive science and discovery centre (www.w5online.co.uk) – the name a zippy way to say 'who, what, where, when, why' – which has over 250 exhibits and daily demonstrations. There's also a twelve-screen Cineworld multiplex on site and a Hollywood Bowl, plus numerous fast-food eateries to keep the family fuelled.

Public Record Office

Looking for your ancestors? Then this is the place to start. A staggering three million documents and 300,000 maps are stored in the archives of the **Public Record Office of Northern Ireland 5** on Titanic Boulevard (PRONI; www.ni direct.gov.uk/proni). Most records date from around 1600 to the present. There is no entry fee, but new visitors must show photo ID to register and use the research facilities.

Newtownards Road

Head west on Queen's Quay, take a left at Station Road then east at Middlepath Street (A2) and follow the road as it veers left and becomes Newtownards Road (A20). You can still get a glimpse of east Belfast's prosperous industrial era at the beginning of this road, where much of the old working-class housing has been preserved. On the left stands **St Patrick's 6** – the 'Shipyard Church' dating from 1833; note the murals close to loyalist hearts and the **Titanic Mural** painted on the gable end at Dee Street, dedicated to the men and women who

lost their lives on that tragic night in 1912. The Banana Block events space (PortView Trade Centre, 310 Newtownards Rd; www.bananablock. org) is a symbol of either gentrification or regeneration, depending on how you look at it (and your budget).

Set within a historic linen mill, it hosts club nights as well as craft and food markets featuring pricey bagels and cakes, fungi and plant workshops, and permanent history displays.

C.S. Lewis

Our route detours north onto Holywood Road to the childhood stomping ground of author C.S. Lewis (1898–1963). The fifth road on the right, **Dundela Avenue**, is where Lewis was born – a blue plaque marks the spot, and now the site of a block of flats. On 47 Sydenham Avenue (third turning after Dundela) is **St Mark's Dundela 7** where Lewis saw his fearsome grandfather preach each Sunday. The house he grew up in, **Little Lea** (in whose attic flourished the youthful imagination that led to Narnia), is a private residence on Circular Road with no public access, also marked by a blue plaque. In 2016, C.S. Lewis Square opened at the intersection of Connswater and Comber Greenways, adorned with seven sculptures of the characters from *The Lion, The Witch and The Wardrobe*. EastSide Visitor Centre sits at its roadside edge. Not Lewis-related but of interest, is the Art Deco building of the Strand Arts Centre and

Cinema (152–154 Holywood Road; www.strandartscentre.com).

Stormont

Retrace the route to Newtownards Road and push east. After about 1.5 miles (2.5km) you reach the gates of the Parliament Buildings at **Stormont** ❽. Opened in 1932, Parliament was designed by Sir Arnold Thornely in Classical Greek style. Its extensive parkland includes jogging trails and children's play areas, as well as the Scottish baronial-style 1830 manor house, known as Stormont Caste.

Public tours operate each day, book online via Eventbrite.

George Best's Belfast

Return the way you came and turn onto Knock Road. Those with an interest in police uniforms and firearms can visit the **Police Museum** ❾ at No. 65 (www.psni.police.uk; by appointment;

free). Around two miles on, turn into Cregagh Road and pass the Museum of Orange Heritage (368 Cregagh Road; www.orangeheritage.co.uk; free). Football fans will be interested in the Protestant working-class **Cregagh Estate** ❿ where you can stay in the childhood home of footballing legend George Best (1946–2005), at No. 16 Burren Way (www.georgebesthouse.com). This modest house was lived in by George's father, Dickie, until his death in 2008, after which it was bought by the local regeneration charity EastSide Partnership. It has since been refurbished with retro interiors to look as it would have done in 1961, with family portraits hung on the walls, George's old school reports scattered across the table and a vintage kitchen.

Return to Cregagh Road and drive (or bus) north onto Woodstock Road, onto Albert Bridge Road and head back into the city.

Eating out

Café at the Museum of Orange Heritage
368B Cregagh Road; tel: 07724 414564.
There are fewer better, or more appropriate, places in which to enjoy a perfectly cooked Ulster Fry than in the café that's part of a museum dedicated to the Orange Order and its culture. Locals and museum visitors chat over cups of tea and traybakes or baked potatoes. Staff are welcoming and there is outdoor seating for sunny days. £

Kamakura East Sushi & Ramen Restaurant
18 Holywood Road;
www.kamakurasushi.co.uk.
One of two Belfast branches of this traditional Japanese restaurant (the other is at Donegall Pass). High-quality, fresh ingredients are used in an extensive menu covering sushi, sashimi, ramen and grill options. Also offers takeout. ££

Linen Lounge at Belfast Metropolitan College
7 Queen's Road; tel: 028-9026 5170.
In the heart of the Titanic Quarter, the food in this fully licensed training restaurant is cooked and served by the collage's hospitality students amid decor recalling the shipyard's history. Open during term time; the prices are cheap, the quality high. £

Bullhouse East
442–446 Newtownards Road;
www.bullhousebrewco.com.
Belfast's family- and dog-friendly Bullhouse Brewing Company opened its first permanent taproom in 2022. Go for the beers, stay for the pizza, made in wood-fired ovens in the garden, which backs onto C.S. Lewis Square. It's very popular so be prepared to wait during peak times. ££

The interlocking basalt columns of the Giant's Causeway.

TOUR 10

Coastal Causeway to Derry

This spectacular 132-mile (212km) route along the Antrim coast encompasses the Giant's Causeway and dramatic rugged cliffs, then swerves inland to the walled city of Derry.

For many, a drive along the Antrim Coast Road, known as the Causeway Coastal Route, to the Giant's Causeway would be enough for one day, and there is the option of taking one of the many bus tours that cover the same route. But for those who want to explore a bit more, head on to Derry (officially called Londonderry, it's the second largest city in Northern Ireland). To make the most of the complete tour, spend a night there and have a proper look round the next morning. Literature buffs should make their last stop Bellaghy for a snoop inside the **Seamus Heaney HomePlace** (see page 96; www.seamusheaneyhome.com). Situated midway between Derry and Belfast, this purpose-built literary and arts

Highlights

- Carrickfergus
- Causeway Coastal Route
- Carrick-a-rede Rope Bridge
- Giant's Causeway
- Bushmills Distillery
- Dunluce Castle
- Derry's walls and Peace Bridge
- Derry's Guildhall

centre could be taken in on a return journey to Belfast.

North of Belfast

Take the A2 north out of the city, through the suburbs of Whiteabbey and Greenisland, and on to **Carrickfergus ❶** (also called Carrick), a market town twelve miles (19km) north along the A2, strung along the northern shore of Belfast Lough. The imposing thirteenth-century **Norman Carrickfergus Castle** (Marine Highway), poised on top of a rock ledge, is still in excellent shape (see page 89). It's a hit with kids, thanks to its visitor centre, portcullis, sea-facing ramparts, and chilling dungeons. Children also love the stained-glass window depicting St Nicholas as Santa Claus, in the twelfth-century parish church of the eponymous saint.

At 11 Antrim Street, **Carrickfergus Museum** (www.midandeastantrim. gov.uk; free) outlines the town's history. About a mile (2km) to the east, the **Andrew Jackson Cottage** (2 Boneybefore; www.midandeastantrim. gov.uk; free) is a reconstruction of the thatched 1750s Ulster-Scots farmhouse home of Andrew Jackson, seventh president of the United States. Beside it is the US Rangers Museum, dedicated to the elite American Army

Tales of Carrickfergus

Carrickfergus, celebrated in song by many, including Van Morrison, has good stories to tell. Its castle was besieged for a year in 1315 by Edward Bruce's Scottish invaders. William of Orange first set foot on Irish soil here on his way to defeat James II at the Battle of the Boyne in 1690. The French briefly captured the town in 1760.

unit that was formed in Carrickfergus in 1942, during World War II.

Pristine beaches

The countryside north of Carrickfergus gives way to rich meadowland and the sleepy seaside town of **Whitehead**, base for the Railway Preservation Society of Ireland, from where occasional steam excursions run. The town nestles at the mouth of the lough, with a seashore walk to the Black Head lighthouse. Beyond the

The Gobbins Cliff Path.

peninsula of **Islandmagee**, with its unspoiled beaches and caves, wraps around Larne Lough. A highlight is the historic **Gobbins cliff path** (Middle Road, www.thegobbinscliffpath.com), a dramatic coastal walk cut into the rock. A 2016 restoration saw the addition of a stainless-steel staircase linking a half-mile path with a new clifftop trail. From here, the road cuts into functional **Larne ❷**, a port with frequent ferries to and from Stranraer in Scotland (70min away). The **Larne Museum and Arts Centre** (2 Victoria Road; tel: 028-2826 2443; free) has displays reflecting the history and heritage of the area.

Causeway Coastal Route

The rewards of continuing along the coast are spectacular kaleidoscopic views of brown moorlands, white limestone, black basalt, red sandstone and blue sea. A notable engineering achievement, the Causeway Coast is explained in the Glenarm Visitor Information Point (Glenarm Marina; www.glenarmtourism.org), located in a renovated former school building. The road, designed in 1834 by Sir Charles Lanyon, opened up an area whose inhabitants had previously

found it easier to travel by sea to Scotland than overland to the rest of Northern Ireland.

Ballygalley

Ballygalley ❸, at the start of the scenic drive, has a 1625 fortified mansion (now a hotel) and, inland, a well-preserved mill and pottery. White Bay is a picnic area around which small fossils can be found. **Glenarm** has a beautiful park adjoining a castle, with a woodland walk, heritage centre, activities and glamping pods (2 Castle Lane; www. glenarmcastle.com). **Carnlough** is home to a fine harbour and a white bridge straddling its main street, built in 1854 to carry limestone from the quarries to waiting boats. The *Londonderry Arms Hotel* retains the charms of an old coaching inn.

The Glens

Next, you reach **Waterfoot**, which is at the entrance to Glenariff Glen, a deep wooded gorge dubbed by Thackeray 'Switzerland in miniature'. Wildflowers carpet the upper glen in spring and early summer, and rustic bridges carry walkers over the Glenariff River, past postcard-pretty waterfalls.

Crashing waves at Ballycastle.

About 1.5 miles (2km) to the north, **Cushendall**, 'capital of the glens', was created largely by a wealthy nineteenth-century landowner, Francis Turnley. His most striking structure was the four-storey red sandstone Curfew Tower, now owned by Bill Drummond of 1980s pop group KLF, and is used as an artists' residence. Just to the north, the thirteenth-century Layde Old Church conceals some ancient vaults. In 1924, the village was one of the first in Ireland to have street lighting. Six miles (10km) further on, you can loop round on the B92 to

Cushendun ❹, a village of attractive white cottages, graceful old houses and friendly pubs, protected by the National Trust.

The Northern Coast

Still following the Causeway Coastal Route, you cross the towering Glendun Viaduct (1839), and just before arriving in Ballycastle, pass the ruins of Bonamargy Friary, founded around 1500. A vault shelters the massive coffins of several MacDonnell chieftains who successfully rebuffed the forces of Queen Elizabeth I.

Ballycastle

The best time to visit **Ballycastle** ❺ is during the Auld Lammas Fair, held at the end of August when this unspoilt town turns into a bustling marketplace. Farmers with strong country accents bring their livestock in from the glens and hundreds of stalls sell souvenirs, bric-a-brac, dulse (dried, edible seaweed) and yellowman (a sweet confectionery, like honeycomb). It's great fun and an authentic folk event. The **Ballycastle Museum** (Castle Street; tel: 028-2076 2942; free) concentrates on the folk history of the glens.

TOUR 10 THE NORTHERN COAST

The Giant's Causeway

The Giant's Causeway Visitor Experience (www.nationaltrust.org.uk) blends into the landscape, ensuring that the indigenous grasses on the roof restore the natural ridgeline and provide a habitat for wildlife. Special environmental features include water-permeable paving and rainwater harvesting. Bypass the centre to visit the stones for free or buy a Visitor Experience ticket for pre-booked parking and use of the centre facilities.

The Giant's Causeway Visitor Experience.

A seafront memorial marks the spot where, in 1898, Guglielmo Marconi first seriously tested wireless telegraphy. He made his historic transmission between here and **Rathlin Island** ❻, eight miles (13km) off the coast towards Scotland. The boomerang-shaped island, whose population has slumped from 2000 to less than 100 since 1850, attracts geologists, botanists and birdwatchers; a reserve (tel: 028-2076 0062) monitors an estimated 250,000 birds of 175 species. There is one pub, a hotel, guesthouse, glamping and a youth hostel – but no police, and no need for any.

A vehicle ferry (www.rathlin-ferry.com; reservations advised) makes the journey from Ballycastle in forty minutes. There's also a high-speed catamaran which cuts the crossing time to 25 minutes, with round-trips available daily.

Carrick-a-Rede Rope Bridge

Carry on along the Causeway Coastal Route, which diverts west off the A2 to the **Carrick-a-Rede Rope Bridge** (119a Whitepark Road, Ballintoy; www.nationaltrust.org.uk), over an 80ft (24m) chasm to an island salmon fishery (see box). It's worth crossing

Exhilarating bridge

The Carrick-a-Rede Rope Bridge provides a novel way to gain an alternative view of the spectacular coastline. Spare a thought for the salmon fishermen who once traversed this chasm, braving a bridge of widely spaced wooden slats and a single rope handrail. Today, you navigate a more substantial suspension bridge with two handrails. Old photographs even show people performing stunts, such as handstands on a chair in the middle and riding across on a bicycle.

the bridge for the view of the crashing waves, but it is a good half-mile (1km) from the car park.

Back on the road past Whitepark Bay is Dunseverick Castle, the crumbling remains of a sixth-century fortress perched on a crag overlooking a fishing harbour. Follow the signs to the Giant's Causeway.

The Giant's Causeway

Dunseverick Castle is at the eastern end of the **Giant's Causeway** ❼, an astonishing assembly, discovered only in 1692, of more than 40,000 basalt

The prismatic shapes of the spectacular Giant's Causeway.

Crossing the Carrick-a-Rede Rope Bridge.

columns, mostly perfect hexagons formed by the cooling of molten lava. The formal approach is via the Giant's Causeway Visitor Experience (www.nationaltrust.org.uk; car park charge included in admission ticket) two miles (3km) north of Bushmills on the B146. The glass-fronted visitor centre is made of locally quarried basalt (see page 91), but paying to visit it is optional, as access to the actual stones is free. A minibus provides wheelchair access to the Causeway. For a small fee anyone can take the shuttlebus, but it is a lovely walk down to the rocks and there are opportunities for longer hikes along the coast.

One of the most pleasant ways to reach the Giant's Causeway is on the **Giant's Causeway and Bushmills Railway** steam train (tel: 028-2073 2844), from Bushmills, which is where our route continues, following the coastal route, the A2.

The world's oldest distillery

The distillery at **Bushmills** ❽ (2 Distillery Road; www.bushmills. eu) a couple of miles away, has the world's oldest whiskey-making licence (1608). Old Bushmills, Black Bush

and Bushmills Malt, made from local barley and the water that flows by in St Columb's Rill, can be tasted after a tour.

About two miles (3km) along the coast road are the romantic remains of **Dunluce Castle** (tel: 028-2073 1938). Poised on a rocky headland, the dramatic fourteenth-century stronghold was featured in HBO's *Game of Thrones*. It was abandoned in 1641, two years after part of the kitchen collapsed into the sea during a storm, carrying many of the servants to their deaths. In the graveyard of the adjacent ruined church are buried

Barrels at Bushmills Distillery.

Derry, on the River Foyle.

sailors from the Spanish Armada galleass *Girona*, wrecked on nearby rocks in 1588. The castle was once owned by Sir Winston Churchill.

Portrush and Portstewart

Next along the coast are two seaside resorts. **Portrush** ❾ is the livelier, with amusement arcades, burger bars, karaoke pubs, souvenir shops, a children's play park, boat trips for sea fishing and viewing the Causeway, and two championship golf courses.

Portstewart is the quieter, a tidy Victorian town with a huge strand, popular with anglers for its excellent beach casting. Long-distance walkers can pick up the North Antrim Coast Path at Portstewart Strand; it forms part of the Ulster Way and extends east for forty miles (64km) to Murlough Bay. The road bypasses **Coleraine**, a busy market and university town.

Portrush pleasures

The resort of Portrush has seashore discovery pools and tanks. For an alternative fun-filled family experience, you can while away a morning or afternoon at Curry's Fun Park (www.currysfunpark.com) formerly the long-established Barry's Amusements, where dodgems and the thrill of the ghost train are the main draws.

The Road to Derry

Continue on the A2 towards Derry City, 37 miles (60km) via the coastal route. On a windswept headland is **Downhill Demesne** ❿ (Castlerock; tel: 028-7084 8728), concealing the ruins of Downhill Castle and Hezlett House. Here, too, is the National Trust-owned **Mussenden Temple**, perched on a cliff, which housed an eccentric bishop's library; it was inspired by the temples of Vesta at Tivoli and Rome. Downhill Forest has lovely walks and waterfalls.

Benone Beach, part of **Magilligan Strand**, is one of Ireland's best, with golf, tennis and heated pools available at its excellent Benone Tourist Complex (tel: 028-7775 0555).

Follow the A2 to Limavady and on to the city of Londonderry/Derry (its name a dispute between nationalists and unionists; officially called Londonderry, many use the shortened version), where you might consider staying the night.

Derry City

Derry ⓫, finely situated on the River Foyle, is famously friendly. Even its sectarian conflicts are far less implacable than Belfast's. The nineteenth-century Scottish historian Thomas Carlyle called it 'the prettiest looking town I have seen in Ireland'. The Troubles may have left scars, but it has been well refurbished. Since

Bogside artists

A good way to experience the political history of the Bogside is to join a tour of the dramatic murals. Guided tours of all thirteen murals, known collectively as 'The People's Gallery', are available and you learn more of the complex history that inspired the artists. You won't hear the stories elsewhere: these are straight from the horse's mouth.

The historic Derry walls.

2011 the city's major public buildings such as St. Columb's Cathedral, the Guildhall, and its museums and churches have emerged from a glow-up programme. The spectacular **Peace Bridge** across the Foyle opened in 2011, linking the west bank with Ebrington Square, a redeveloped military parade ground now converted into an arts hub hosting concerts and other events. In 2013 it was named a UK City of Culture during which it trumpeted its artistic credentials to a wider world, leaving an important legacy. The TV comedy series *Derry Girls* (2018–2022), set during the Troubles in the early 1990s, introduced the city to a new generation of fans.

The city's growth was financed by London guilds, which in 1613 began creating the last walled city in Europe. You can see traces of its former economic confidence in the ornamental facades of the old shirt-making factories, which provided the city with its livelihood. The walls, 20ft (6m) thick and complete with watchtowers and cannon, are marvellously intact and you can hear the full history on a guided walking tour (www.derrycitytours.com).

Two seventeenth-century sieges failed to breach the walls. Some say

A message painted on the wall of a house in Bogside.

YOU ARE NOW ENTERING FREE DERRY
PALESTINE, THAILAND, SRI LANKA, AFGHANISTAN, IRAQ.......
NO MORE BLOODY SUNDAYS

Literary detour

Take the A6 out of Derry into the mid-Ulster countryside for 38 miles (65km) to the village of Bellaghy, where the late poet and Nobel laureate Seamus Heaney (1939–2013) grew up. Heaney's poetry was massively inspired by the surrounding countryside and frequently evoked rural life. **Seamus Heaney HomePlace** (45 Main Street; www.seamusheaneyhome.com) is a sleek arts centre with a permanent exhibition on Heaney's life, a café, a theatre and a full cultural programme. Housed in a former police barracks that has been reimagined as a Modernist space, the centre enjoys stunning rural views. Its location, a 45-minute drive from either Derry or Belfast, makes it a convenient day-trip from either city.

Inside Derry's Tower Museum.

the city still has a siege mentality, a theory reinforced by the IRA's daubed slogan 'You are now entering Free Derry'. This was the name given to the Bogside (see page 95), a densely populated Catholic housing estate, when its inhabitants barricaded it against the police in 1969. Their grievances were old ones. For more on the civil rights movement and the story of Bloody Sunday, visit the **Museum of Free Derry** (55 Glenfada Park, Bogside; www.museumoffreederry.org).

The most famous battle took place in 1689, when the Catholic forces of James II blockaded the Protestant supporters of William of Orange for fifteen weeks, almost forcing them into submission. Around 7000 of the 30,000 people packed within the city's walls died of disease or starvation. One member of the besieged garrison chillingly recorded the selling prices of horseflesh, dogs' heads, cats, and rats 'fattened by eating the bodies of the slain Irish'. The city's eventual relief is depicted in the memorial window of St Columb's Cathedral, a graceful seventeenth-century Anglican church.

Tower Museum

The **Tower Museum** (Union Hall Place; tel: 028-7137 2411) skilfully uses audiovisuals and photography to tell the city's turbulent history from both sides of the sectarian divide.

Around the city

Streets from the city's original four gates converge on The Diamond, a square-shaped marketplace at the top of steep Shipquay Street. At the bottom, the rejuvenated **Guildhall** (Guildhall Square; www.guildhallderry.com; free) is a civic centre and events space, offering prebooked guided tours and a tourist information point with touchscreen displays explaining the building's special features.

Behind the Guildhall is Derry Quay, celebrated in song by thousands of emigrants who sailed down the Foyle, bound for a new life in America.

Eating out

BALLYCASTLE
The Cellar Restaurant
11b The Diamond;
www.cellarballycastle.com.
Plenty of atmosphere abounds at this cosy restaurant with its vaulted ceiling and string of eating spaces. Seafood is the speciality, but meat lovers will not be disappointed by the excellent local beef. £££

BUSHMILLS
The Bushmills Inn
9 Dunluce Road;
www.bushmillsinn.com.
Ever-popular nineteenth-century coaching inn where traditional dishes are given the Bushmills twist. The Sunday carvery is popular as is the afternoon tea, or opt for Guinness and oysters at the hotel's *Gas Bar*. £££

Tartine
Distillers Arms, 140 Main Street;
www.distillersarms.com.
A contemporary restaurant in the former distillery pub. The menu features succulent local venison, lamb, steak and seafood along with some vegan dishes. There are good-value Sunday lunch and early-bird menus as well as options for the kids. £££

CARNLOUGH
Londonderry Arms Hotel
20 Harbour Road;
www.londonderryarmshotel.com.
A traditional inn where the dining choice ranges from bar meals in the *Coach House Bistro* to afternoon tea in the Frances Anne Drawing Room. All the menus showcase the finest local ingredients; finish off the meal with a tipple from the various malts, blends and vintages in the *Arkle Whiskey Bar*. £££

Twilight Coffee & Bunkhouse
54–56 Harbour Road;
www.twilightantrimcoast.com.
Gorgeous views and a friendly welcome await guests, including dogs, at *Twilight*. Brunch is a highlight, but you can also simply grab an artisan coffee and a home-baked pastry. Expect vegan faves like avo toast as well as gluten-free options, plus a bowl of water for your four-legged friend. £

CUSHENDALL
Harry's Restaurant
10 Mill Street;
www.harryscushendall.co.uk.
A good stop for a quick bite, with friendly staff serving pub-style food. Great-value dishes include freshly battered fish, burgers, salads and sandwiches; the portions are generous, and the atmosphere is friendly. Don't miss the mid-week specials. ££

DERRY
Browns Bonds Hill
1 Bonds Hill;
www.brownsbondshill.com.
This well-respected restaurant has garnered accolades for its fine-dining menu, impeccable service and unpretentious, relaxed ambience. £££

GIANT'S CAUSEWAY
The Brasserie
Gray's, 306 Whitepark Road;
www.graysbushmills.com.
Perfectly placed on the Causeway Coastal Route, just minutes from the Giant's Causeway is elegant restaurant *The Brasserie*. Head chef Simon Turner focuses on Northern Irish produce such as Kilkeel haddock and Glenarm Estate steak and beef. In summer you can eat alfresco on the terrace overlooking the coast. £££

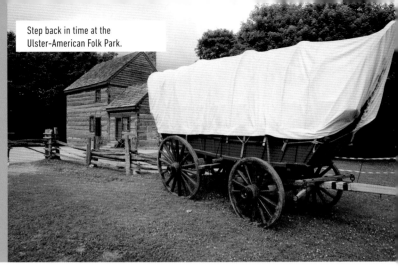

Step back in time at the Ulster-American Folk Park.

TOUR 11

Across three counties

Covering 150 miles (240km), this one-day, cross-county route provides a whistlestop tour of some of Northern Ireland's most popular attractions, plus a brief trip into the Republic.

County Tyrone, in the heart of Northern Ireland, is home to the majestic Sperrin Mountains, forests and rivers, and is favoured by hill walkers and anglers. Fermanagh is riddled with waterways, the most visited being Lough Erne. The northernmost point in Ireland is in the Republic – don't forget euros as you cross the border – in County Donegal. It's an open, unspoiled region, popular with holidaymakers.

If you have time, consider staying overnight along the route.

County Tyrone

Thirteen miles (21km) southwest of **Derry City**, in County Tyrone on the A5, is **Strabane** ❶, a border town paired with Lifford on the Donegal

> ### Highlights
> - Ulster-American Folk Park
> - Lough Erne
> - Marble Arch Caves
> - Lough Navar Forest Park
> - Castle Caldwell
> - Belleek
> - Donegal

side. The Tourist Information Centre (1 Railway Street; tel: 028-7138 4444) has details of attractions in the town and surrounding area. In Dergalt, two miles (3km) southeast, signposted off the B47, is a whitewashed cottage, ancestral home of former US president Woodrow Wilson (tel: 028-7138 4444; free).

Recreation of an old Ulster street, Ulster-American Folk Park.

Sion Mills, three miles (5km) south of Strabane, is a planned model village whose name betrays its origins. The linen-workers' cottages are charming. The parish Church of the Good Shepherd is a striking Italian-style edifice, contrasting with the Modernist St Teresa's Catholic Church, whose slate facade depicts the Last Supper by Irish sculptor Oisin Kelly (1915–1981). Continue along the A5 to the Ulster-American Folk Park.

Ulster-American Folk Park

Thomas Mellon, who emigrated to Pittsburgh at the age of five in 1818, went on to found a great industrial and banking empire. His descendants, having traced their family roots to four miles (6km) north of Omagh, off the A5, endowed the **Ulster-American Folk Park ❷** (www.ulsteramericanfolkpark. org) on the site at Camphill. An indoor exhibit recreates the main street of an Ulster town a century ago, its hardware shop displaying foot warmers and lamp wicks, its medical hall containing Bishop's Granular Effervescent Citrate of Magnesia. A replica of an emigrant ship links the continents. History comes to life on special occasions (such as US

Independence Day) when actors recreate battles, while others demonstrate traditional cooking and craft skills.

The Mellon Centre for Migration Studies on the site has a reference library open for research. There is also a good café and picnic areas.

County town

As you drive into **Omagh ❸**, the religious fragmentation of Northern Ireland is apparent in the abundance of churches. The joining of the rivers Camowen and Drumragh to form the Strule makes the location pleasant enough, but Omagh is more a town for living in than for visiting.

Locals still recall the day in August 1998 when 29 people, including a woman pregnant with twins, were killed in a Real IRA car-bomb explosion. Some three hundred others were injured in what was the single biggest atrocity of the Troubles. The quiet and reflective Omagh Memorial Garden (2 Drumragh Avenue) is a poignant tribute to the victims.

Enniskillen Castle.

County Fermanagh

From Omagh take the A32 to the county town of Fermanagh, **Enniskillen ❹**, a Protestant stronghold since Tudor times, built on an island between two channels of the River Erne as it flows from Upper to Lower **Lough Erne**. Although something of a traffic bottleneck, in summer you can escape it all by taking one of the pleasure boats that ply the lakes (MV *Kestrel*, Round 'O' Jetty, Brook Park; www.ernetours.com). Three miles (5km) north of the town at the A32/B82 junction, **Devenish Island** is the best known of the lough's 97 islands for its elaborate and well-preserved tower, which can be climbed by internal ladders. Close by are the decorative ruins of the twelfth-century Augustinian Abbey of St Mary. In June

2013, the G8 summit was held in the *Lough Erne Resort*, a five-star hotel and golf resort. Among the world leaders who stayed there for several days were former US president Barack Obama and Russian president Vladimir Putin.

Enniskillen town

The town's strategic importance is shown by **Enniskillen Castle** (www.enniskillencastle.co.uk), the earliest parts dating from the fifteenth century. The castle houses the Fermanagh County Museum, focusing on local history, and the Inniskillings Museum, with exhibits on military history and weaponry. In 2022, a memorial to the twelve people killed by an IRA bomb in 1987 was installed on a wall of what is now the Clinton Centre, which was built on the site of the bomb on Belmore Street.

Enniskillen, Ireland's only island town, is rich in small bakeries and butchers' shops, particularly O'Doherty's, home of the famous Fermanagh Black Bacon (3 Belmore Street; www.blackbacon.com). You'll find a neighbourly atmosphere in *Blakes of the Hollow* on Church Street (tel: 028-6632 2143), one of the province's most famous Victorian pubs.

Monumental view

If you have the energy to climb 108 steps to the top of Cole's Monument in Forthill Park, Enniskillen, the reward is a stunning view of the surrounding area from the viewing platform (tickets from the Fermanagh Visitor Information Centre, Enniskillen Castle; www.fermanaghlakelands.com).

Castle Archdale

A centre for ecotours, Castle Archdale Country Park (Countryside Centre: tel: 028-6862 1588; free) on the east shore has pony trekking, boating, bike hire, fishing rod rental, a tearoom and 230 acres (90 hectares) of parkland with some wonderful walks and cycle rides. There is also a caravan and camp site. A ferry departs from Castle Archdale marina for White Island, famed for its twelfth-century church, with eight mysterious pagan statues.

Two miles (3km) east of Enniskillen on the A4 is Ireland's finest classical mansion, **Castle Coole** (www.national trust.org.uk).

Marble Arch Caves

Set in the heart of a UNESCO Global Geopark, the **Marble Arch Caves** ❺ (Marlbank Road; www.marble archcaves.co.uk) are one of the most visited sights in Ireland. Located twelve miles (20km) southwest of Enniskillen, the caves are reached by following the A4 southwest for three miles (5km), then branching off on the A32 and following signposts towards Swanlinbar. This extensive network of limestone chambers conceals remarkable stalactites. A 75-minute tour includes an underground boat journey. There's also a café and a shop.

Florence Court

Four miles (6km) east of the caves is a beautiful eighteenth-century mansion, **Florence Court** ❻ (www.national trust.org.uk) set on a sustainable estate and gardens. In the interior are fine rococo plasterwork and antique furniture. The grounds include an icehouse, a water-powered sawmill, a walled garden and a kitchen garden restored to its 1930s heyday.

Lough Erne

Rejoin the A32 and take the A4 back to Enniskillen for a tour of Lower Lough Erne by road or boat. Follow the A46 north to Tully, with a well-preserved seventeenth-century castle and gardens. Inland from here, take the B81 to Derrygonnelly and follow signs for a beautiful seven-mile (11km) drive through wind-tousled heath, bog, woodland, coniferous forest and open water – welcome to **Lough Navar Forest Park** ❼. There are panoramic views of the lough, Donegal Bay and the Blue Stack and Sperrin mountains from the Magho Cliffs, which rise to 1000ft (304m). As well as car parking there is a picnic area, viewpoints and four walking trails. Navar is part of the Cuilcagh Lakelands Geopark (www.cuilcagh lakelands.org). Straddling the border between Northern Ireland and the Republic, Cuilcagh is one of only four transnational geoparks in the world. It gained its title as a UNESCO Global Geopark due to its significance as a region of geological heritage, with international significance.

Back on the A46, you can take a small detour north at Rosscor to join the A47 to visit another of the geopark's sites, **Castle Caldwell Forest** ❽ five miles (8km) east. This ancient

TOUR 11 LOUGH ERNE

Lough Navar Forest Park sits on the shores of lower Lough Erne.

Making the finishing touches at Belleek pottery.

woodland by the rugged shoreline of Lower Lough Erne is scored with walking trails and a jetty as well as the ruins of a sixteenth-century castle. Return along the A47 to Belleek.

Belleek

The border touches the River Erne again at **Belleek ❾**. The village is famous for its lustrous pottery, manufactured from felspar imported from Norway. The Belleek Visitor Centre (3 Main Street; www.belleek. com; free) at the distinctive 1893 factory building is a popular attraction and visitors love ending a pottery tour with a visit to the quaint tearoom, where food and drinks are served on delicate Belleek tableware.

Just one of the many bars in Donegal.

County Donegal

Leaving Belleek, push north to County Donegal, where you reach the Republic of Ireland. The road signs now show kilometres instead of miles and the currency is the euro, not the sterling of the UK. Take the N3 to the bypassed **Ballyshannon**, then the N15 to the lively county town of **Donegal ❿**, with a busy triangular 'diamond' market square, congested with tourist traffic all summer. The town's **castle**, once an O'Donnell stronghold, was redesigned by planters who took over the land after the O'Donnells were deported in the 'Flight of the Earls' at the turn of the seventeenth century. In the now-ruined Franciscan abbey, on the Eske estuary, monks compiled *The Annals of the Four Masters* in the 1630s, tracing Ireland's ancient history.

Apart from tourism, the weaving and making up of tweeds is the main industry, and Magee (www.magee 1866.com), the largest shop, is the principal outlet. A mile (1.6km) south on the R267, Donegal Craft Village (www.donegalcraftvillage. com) is a creative collective of craft and art studios, where you can pick up handmade gifts, ranging from jewellery to prints and pottery, and meet the makers. Its *Aroma* coffee shop is a great place in which to take time out.

Taking the N15 out of Donegal, and passing Lough Eske to the west, the route nudges into the rugged, dramatic **Barnesmore Gap**. Continue past Lough Mourne, through Ballybofey and north on the N13 to **Letterkenny** ⑪, a vibrant town on the River Swilly, whose most prominent landmark is the cathedral, built in neo-Gothic style by local masons, using Donegal stone.

Eating out

BELLEEK
The Thatch
20 Main Street; tel: 028-6865 8181. This picture-perfect coffee shop is housed in the only thatched building remaining in the county, dating from the eighteenth century. It has been serving home-made food since the early 1900s. Today's options include the likes of paninis, soups, frys, toasties and scones with jam and cream. £

DONEGAL
Aroma
Donegal Craft Village; www.donegalcraftvillage.com. Everything is prepared and baked daily on the premises at this coffee shop at the craft centre. Plenty of choice for a coffee break, lunch or afternoon tea; particularly good are the Mexican *chimichangas* and *quesadillas*, while it's famous for its brown bread and cakes for good reason. ££

The Olde Castle Seafood Bar
Tirchonaill Street, Donegal Town; www.oldecastlebar.com. Housed in a charming old building, this leading seafood restaurant has won numerous awards over the years, including Best Gastro Pub Ulster 2023. Fish is a speciality, but meat-eaters can enjoy the likes of Wicklow venison pie. Push the boat out with the seafood platter for two. £££

ENNISKILLEN
The Firehouse
26 Townhall Street; www.thefirehouse.org.uk. This bar and grill offers a fresh and varied selection of meals throughout the day, from lunches and pizzas to evening meals and cocktails. Steaks, pasta and seafood are accompanied by plant-based options such as the vegan tofu kebab. £££

LETTERKENNY
Lemon Tree Restaurant
32–34 Courtyard Shopping Centre, Lower Main Street; www.thelemontreerestaurant.com. An inviting, family-run place offering an excellent modern, seasonal menu. Produce is sourced locally and sustainably, and the breads, pastries, pastas and desserts are made fresh on site. Save space for the delicious desserts and cheeseboard. £££

OMAGH
Grants
29 George's Street; tel: 028-8225 0900. Established in 1997 and known for its attentive and friendly staff, the interior is full of character and the menu filled with well-crafted Irish and globally inspired dishes, with the likes of duck-breast steak burgers followed by brownies for dessert. ££

STRABANE
Oysters
37 Patrick Street; www.oystersrestaurant.co.uk. Classic dishes with a contemporary twist at a popular, award-winning restaurant, which has garnered multiple accolades for its excellent food and service. Ingredients are locally sourced, with suppliers listed on the website. £££

The Mourne Mountains meet the sea at Newcastle.

TOUR 12

Armagh and the Mourne Mountains

Covering 120 miles (194km), this is a one-day tour of captivating contrasts: from outer city suburbs to stunning mountain scenery.

County Armagh is called the 'Apple Orchard of Ireland', known for its National Trust properties, neat villages and country lanes. As we move into County Down, the Mourne Mountains offer wonderful outdoor recreation and the most stunning scenery Northern Ireland has to offer.

Road to Armagh

Take the A1 south from Belfast to the lively city of **Lisburn** ❶, which has an informative **Museum and Irish Linen Centre** (Market Square; www.lisburnmuseum.com; free).

From Lisburn take the A3 towards Armagh, making a short detour to **Lough Neagh Discovery Centre** ❷ (www.oxfordisland.com; free) on Oxford Island, a designated National

Highlights

- Lough Neagh Discovery Centre
- Armagh
- Gosford Forest Park
- Mourne Mountains
- Rostrevor

Nature Reserve. Birdwatchers and walkers love its reedbeds, wildflower meadows and wildlife ponds. The lough is seventeen miles long by eleven miles wide (27km by 18km), the largest inland sheet of water in the British Isles.

Because of its marshy edges, it has few access points – one reason it has remained one of Western Europe's most important bird habitats. The best way to explore is by boat. Abháinn Cruises (www.abhainn cruises.com) offers a Lough Neagh Cruise, taking in the lough's many features. Lough Neagh Sailing Club, based at Kinnego Marina, offers taster sessions for ages eight and upwards (www.loughneagh sailingclub.org).

Armagh City

Continue on the A3 to **Armagh** ❸, which symbolises many of Northern Ireland's past conflicts. Its two striking cathedrals – one Protestant, one Catholic and both called St Patrick's – sit on opposite hills. A Georgian Festival, each Autumn, includes architectural walks, ghost tours and history talks.

At one end of an oval mall is a classical courthouse, at the other a former jailhouse. The Ionic-pillared **County Museum** (The Mall; www. visitarmagh.com; free) contains local artefacts, paintings, and collections on military history and railways.

The **Palace Demesne** covers seventy acres (28 hectares) of beautiful parkland, where the palace building,

> ## Discovering planets
>
> Armagh's Observatory and Planetarium (College Hill; www.armagh.space) is hugely popular with children as well as adults, with astronomical dome shows bookable specifically for under-fives. Touch a meteorite in the exhibition area and interact with a scale model of the solar system in the outdoor astropark. A sensory room is filled with interactive toys, for children with additional sensory needs.

once the residence of the Archbishops of the Church of Ireland from 1770 to 1975, and stables, designed in 1768, take centre stage.

Today, it is a public park with a wide variety to see and do; walk through the serene back meadows, the formal gardens or the garden of the senses or enjoy one of the many events that take place here throughout the year.

This way to the cathedrals.

The Mourne Mountains shrouded in mist.

Mourne Mountains

On the A28 southeast of Armagh is Markethill, where nearby **Gosford Forest Park** ❹ (tel: 028-3755 1277; free) features a turreted mock-Norman castle. Continue on the A28 to Newry, the gateway to the Mountains of Mourne. Equidistant between Dublin and Belfast, the city of **Newry** ❺ was bound to prosper once the peace process began and the motorway was extended north and south.

The Newry and Mourne Museum and the tourist information centre are both in the restored sixteenth-century **Bagenal's Castle** (Castle Street; www.visitmournemountains.co.uk; free).

Moody Mournes

The Mournes are 'young' mountains, and their chameleon qualities attract hikers and walkers. One moment the granite is grey, the next pink. You walk by an isolated farmhouse, and suddenly you are in the middle of a wilderness. One minute, the Mournes justify all the songs written about them; the next, they become plain scrubland and unexceptional hills. The weather has a lot to do with this variety.

Five miles (8km) southeast of Newry along the dual carriageway is the pretty seaside resort of **Warrenpoint**, celebrated for Blues on the Bay each May, one of the finest blues festivals in the UK. The soulful event attracts thousands of visitors and sees the music spill out onto the street. A few minutes around the coast, **Rostrevor** ❻, sheltered by a ring of high hills, is smaller but prettier with a Victorian atmosphere.

A steep half-mile (0.8km) walk up the slopes of **Slievemartin** (1595ft/486m) brings you to Cloghmore, a 'big stone' supposedly hurled by an Irish giant at a rival Scot. The geological explanation is more mundane, having to do with glacial drift.

Skirting round the Mourne Mountains, you pass fourteenth-century Greencastle – a detour on the Carlingford Lough ferry (www.carlingfordferry.com) from here chugs to Co Lough in the Republic. Otherwise, push on to the active fishing village of **Kilkeel** ❼, capital of the so-called 'Kingdom of Mourne'. Its idyllic location between mountain and sea makes it an ideal base from which to explore the peaks.

Brontës and Banbridge

The B27, running north from Kilkeel, takes us through the heart of the mountains. Off the B27, the remote **Silent Valley Mountain Park** cradles a large dam, which supplies Belfast and County Down with water. This beautiful, tranquil spot is ideal for picnics and has an information centre.

Turn north at Hilltown onto the B25, and take the B7 at Rathfriland to Ballroney for the **Brontë Homeland Interpretative Centre** ❽ (Church Hill Road, Rathfriland; tel: 028-4062 3322; group booking only by prior arrangement), a trail invented to capitalise on the fact that Patrick Brontë, father of Charlotte, Emily and Anne, was born nearby.

Join the A50 at Moneyslane and drive to **Banbridge** ❾, with its polar bear memorial to Captain Crozier, discoverer of the Northwest Passage. Just outside Banbridge on the A1 is the huge Bridgewater Park shopping centre, packed with a mix of big names and high-street stores.

Heading in the direction of Belfast, our tour finishes just off the A1 at **Hillsborough** ❿, packed with antique shops and pubs, and rich in Georgian architecture. It's home to Hillsborough Castle, in the Georgian country-house style, where you can tour the state rooms and gardens and see where the Royal Family stay when visiting Northern Ireland (www.hrp.org.uk/hillsborough-castle).

Eating out

ARMAGH
Embers
7 Market Street;
www.embersrestaurant.co.uk.
A friendly neighbourhood haunt that offers everything from cooked breakfasts and lunch specials at the laidback coffeehouse to evening meals at its more formal restaurant. The former serves excellent coffee, freshly baked cakes and sandwiches, while the latter has an extensive grill bar and family-friendly menu. ££

BANBRIDGE
Blend & Batch
104 Newry Street;
www.blendxbatch.com.
A blend of the best roasted coffee in town with home-style batch cooking in a sleek contemporary setting. From breakfast to lunch and on to afternoon cakes, you can't go far wrong. ££

HILLSBOROUGH
The Parson's Nose
48 Lisburn Street; www.ballooinns.com.
This charming and much-loved pub-restaurant conjures up the perfect old-world inn: roaring fires, stags' heads and low-vaulted ceilings. The most desirable food is inspired by local traditions and supports artisan suppliers. £££

WARRENPOINT
The Whistledown Hotel
6 Seaview;
www.thewhistledownhotel.com.
One of the most popular places to eat in town, whether it's for a simple lunch or a special treat. The theme is modern European food with an Irish twist. As well as the *Whistledown Bistro*, there's also *Finn's*, with its bar snacks and lunch specials, and *Meabh's*, the hotel lounge. ££

Raymie's Seafood Bar and Grill
4 Duke Street; tel: 028-4175 4292.
This family-run restaurant has a loyal local following for its excellent seafood and grills, all sourced from the region. Vegans and vegetarians are well catered for – and everything is prepared using the freshest ingredients. ££

Ulster Transport Museum.

TOUR 13
Around the Ards Peninsula

Covering around 115 miles (185km), this one-day tour explores every aspect of this area of outstanding scenic beauty with its rich heritage, history and culture.

The Ards Peninsula, 23 miles (37km) long, provides an excellent focus for a tour. North is the Gold Coast, with seaside resorts and excellent beaches, south is Portaferry where the journey continues via a ferry to attractive towns such as Downpatrick and Newcastle. To the west the road traverses the coast dotted with little fishing ports while east it follows both sides of Strangford Lough to discover a host of wildlife habitats.

Highlights

- Ulster Folk Museum
- Gold Coast beaches
- Mount Stewart
- Exploris
- Strangford Lough
- Newcastle

The Gold Coast

The A2 from Belfast city centre to Bangor runs through what locals describe as the 'Gold Coast'. **George Best Belfast City Airport** on this road is just a few minutes' drive from the heart of the city. Just past the airport,

the attractive, residential town of **Holywood ❶** is sprinkled with good restaurants, cafés and craft shops. Only a fifteen-minute drive from the city centre, along Belfast Lough, it already begins to feel like the countryside. This is stockbroker country, where lush lawns meet mature woodland. Hillside sites, overlooking the shipping lanes, have traditionally lured a well-heeled crowd. **Cultra**, six miles (10km) this side of Bangor, has leafy lanes, splendid houses and the resplendent *Culloden Estate and Spa*. Yachting, golf and horse riding are popular pastimes here.

At Cultra are the **Ulster Folk Museum** (www.ulsterfolkmuseum.org) and the **Ulster Transport Museum** ❷ (www.ulstertransportmuseum. org), two of Northern Ireland's most popular tourist attractions, separated by the A2 Belfast Road. The former is an outdoor 'living museum', in which farmhouses, cottages, churches and mills have been painstakingly reconstructed, often brick by brick, and guides dressed in authentic period costume play the roles of shopkeepers and doctors.

The latter features old vehicles, including a made-in-Belfast DeLorean car, and an RMS *Titanic* exhibition.

Before reaching Bangor, a signposted detour on the B20 takes in the beaches of Helen's Bay, the nearby wooded **Crawfordsburn Country Park** (tel: 028-9185 3621; free), and the pretty village of Crawfordsburn with its historic *Old Inn*, established 1614 and still a place to stay.

Bangor

Bangor ❸, a popular Victorian seaside resort, is noted for its abbey and water-front views. Granted city status in 2022, it is awash with fast-paced regeneration, with the seafront abodes in front of the marina still in need of attention. Planning approval has been granted for many derelict buildings and development work continues to breathe fresh life into the area, albeit slowly. The expensively rejuvenated seafront with its marina full of yachts and cruisers is the main draw for day-trippers. The **North Down Museum** (Town Hall, Bangor Castle; www.andculture.org.uk; free) tells the history of the area from the

Ulster Folk Museum.

TOUR 13 THE GOLD COAST

Bangor Marina has berths for over six hundred vessels.

Bronze Age. It is a busy town with a weekly open-air market, plenty of pubs, restaurants and parks. The best beach is nearby Ballyholme Bay.

South of Bangor on the A21 towards Newtownards is the **Somme Museum** (233 Bangor Road; www.somme association.com/visit/somme-museum), with a reconstructed front-line trench from the World War I battle, on the first

Coastal detour

The A2, southeast from Bangor, traces the coastal side of the peninsula. It's worth taking a detour to the pretty seaside village of **Groomsport** to see the two 400-year-old fishermen's cottages along Cockle Row. **Donaghadee** is notable for its colourful harbour and lighthouse, summer boat trips and tours of the Copeland Distillery on Manor Street, producer of whiskey, rum and gin. The twisting road wiggles past a string of quieter beaches at Ballywalter and Ballyhalbert, and the fishing port of **Portavogie**.

day of which more than two thousand Ulster volunteer soldiers died.

Newtownards

Sprawling **Newtownards** ❹, at the head of **Strangford Lough**, is an old seventeenth-century market town. Today, it's a bustling shopping centre with a blend of traditional shops, a fine sandstone town hall and a covered shopping centre. Overlooking the town on the top of Scrabo Hill is Scrabo Tower (Scrabo Country Park; www.discovernorthernireland.com), a nineteenth-century memorial to the third marquess of Londonderry, offering splendid vistas of the lough and the soft-hilled countryside.

It was a location for the 2014 film *Dracula Untold*.

Strangford Lough

Take the A20 along the east shore of the lough to **Mount Stewart** ❺ (www.nationaltrust.org.uk), an eighteenth-century Neoclassical house with a string of fine gardens and a mild microclimate that fosters delicate plants untypical of the area. The gardens are peppered with statues of griffins, satyrs and heraldic lions. The Temple of the Winds, an eighteenth-century octagonal folly in the grounds, offers a splendid view of the water. Within the grounds of Mount Stewart, take the time to follow the looped walking trails to appreciate the scale of the lough and its wildlife. Family activities include seasonal storytelling events for children, craft workshops and gardening masterclasses.

East shore

South on the A20, the charming village of **Greyabbey** has one of the most complete Cistercian abbeys in Ireland (www.friendsoftheabbey.co.uk; free). Dating from 1193, its remains are an impressive example of early Gothic architecture. Don't miss the medieval herb garden.

Travel to the tip of the peninsula to **Portaferry**, where you'll find **Exploris** ❻ (Castle Street; www.explorisni.com), Northern Ireland's only sea aquarium and seal sanctuary. Here, you need to board the regular car ferry from the town, which takes a picturesque ten-minute slanted course to beautiful **Strangford** ❼. Near Strangford is the eighteenth-century Georgian mansion **Castle Ward** (www.nationaltrust.org.uk), once the home of the lord of Bangor and now a National Trust property.

Castle Ward was also used as a filming location for HBO's *Game of Thrones*. There are wildfowl in the 700-acre (280-hectare) grounds.

Follow the Coast

Take the A2 south from Strangford, which follows the coast passing through **Ardglass** ❽, where a smattering of ruined castles hints at its strategic importance in the Middle Ages. A stopover at Cloghy Rocks is a great place for viewing seals when the

Strangford Lough

The lough, one of Europe's most important wildlife sites, has more than 2000 species of marine animal. Its wetlands support some 25,000 wildfowl and 50,000 waders. Species of tern arrive in summer, and in winter the lough is thought to support 75 percent of the world's Brent geese. Ireland's largest colony of common seals breed here and 30ft (9m) -long basking sharks are sometimes spotted in the lough's entrance.

tide is right. At Clough continue on the A2 as the road almost comes back on itself heading towards Newcastle. This stretch passes Dundrum Castle, Ireland's finest Anglo-Norman castle. **Dundrum** village is a source of wonderful local seafood with an excellent pub-restaurant in which to enjoy it (see page 113).

The Victorian seaside resort of **Newcastle** ❾, where the **Mountains of Mourne** do, as the Percy French ballad describes, 'run down to the sea', is famous for the **Royal County Down**

Birdlife on Strangford Lough.

The sea inlet of Strangford Lough.

Golf Club (www.royalcountydown. org), rated the best course in the world in 2023 by *Golf Digest* magazine. The town, which has a fine sandy beach, is small and picturesque with the 2796ft (850m) peaks of Slieve Donard forming a perfect backdrop. It's a great place to stop and explore, with fish-and-chip shops and ice-cream parlours providing the sustenance and go-karting, crazy golf and pedalos, the fun.

Downpatrick

Take the A50 five miles (8km) inland from Newcastle to Castlewellan, then continue east on the A25 to **Downpatrick ❿**. The name is a marriage of Patrick, this island's patron saint, and the Irish for fort (*dún*). You can follow Patrick's story in a superb exhibition at the **St Patrick Centre** (Market Street; www.saintpatrickcentre.com) located beside his grave. Many people picnic near here by the healing waters of the bathhouses at Struell's St Patrick's Wells. Also in Downpatrick is the excellent **Down County Museum** (www.downcountymuseum.com; free)

showcasing the region's heritage in a 1798 jailhouse.

West Shore

From Downpatrick take the A22 back along the scenic west shore of Strangford Lough, a conservation area, noted for myriad islands, most of which are sunken drumlins, the smooth glacial hillocks that characterise the landscape.

Mahee Island, accessible by bridge, has the remains of Nendrum Abbey (tel: 028-9082 3207; free), thought ot have been founded in the fifth

Steam railway

A hundred yards or so away from the St Patrick Centre is the atmospheric **Downpatrick and County Down Steam Railway** (www.downrail.co.uk), the only full-size heritage railway in Ireland, which excites children as much as it does steam enthusiasts on its two-mile (3km) jaunt. It runs at weekends in season, as well as special occasions such as Easter, Halloween and Christmas.

century, and destroyed by Vikings in AD 974. Castle Espie Wetland Centre (78 Ballydrain Road; www.wwt.org.uk/wetland-centres/castle-espie) is the base for Ireland's largest population of ducks, geese and swans. Activities and events include 'Meet the Keeper' and guided woodland walks.

Comber ⑪, nine miles (14km) southeast of Belfast at the head of Strangford Lough, was a linen town and still has a working mill. The town centre retains its old character with single-storey cottage shops. From Comber, the A22 merges onto the A20 and leads back to the city centre.

Fishing at Donaghadee.

TOUR 13 WEST SHORE

Eating out

COMBER
Old Post Office
191 Killinchy Road, Lisbane; www.opocafe.co.uk.
On the Comber to Killyleagh road, in a listed 1840s building, this quaint tearoom near Strangford Lough serves well-priced food, from hearty breakfasts to three-course lunches and afternoon tea. £

DONAGHADEE
Grace Neill's
33 High Street; www.graceneills.com. Established in 1611, this historic pub offers lashings of character and atmosphere, serving good-value traditional dishes from seafood and steak to a vegan curry. It's a favourite with both locals and visitors. ££

DUNDRUM
Bucks Head Inn
77–79 Main Street; tel: 028-4375 1868. Renowned for its warm welcome, this cosy bar has an open fire, while the restaurant makes the most of the seasonal produce, especially the local Killough Bay oysters and mussels and Kilkeel prawns. ££

HOLYWOOD
Fontana
61 High Street; www.fontanarestaurant.co.uk. Winner of a Michelin Bib Gourmand award, this is a real neighbourhood favourite that's stood the test of time. The menus (a la carte, set, vegetarian, vegan and kids') all make use of local, fresh ingredients. £££

NEWCASTLE
Hugh McCann's
119–21 Central Promenade; www.hughmccanns.com. Nestled in a great location with stunning mountain and sea views, this family-owned restaurant-bar is ideal for a light lunch or something more substantial. ££

STRANGFORD
The Cuan
6–12 The Square, Strangford. Freshly prepared and locally sourced, the food here is served in an elegant yet cosy setting, with carefully chosen ingredients reflecting the seasons. The seafood dishes and desserts are top notch. Open for breakfast, lunch and dinner. ££

Horseriding at Downhill beach.

Popular race meetings are held at Down Royal Racecourse.

TRIP TIPS
Active pursuits

Northern Ireland has such diverse terrain it would be hard to match the quality and range of active pursuits. Loughs, rivers and coastal waters offer second-to-none watersports and fishing, while mountains and cliffs provide an adventure playground for climbers and walkers. Multi-activity centres across the counties have a host of challenging pursuits such as canoeing, abseiling, kayaking, rock climbing, archery and lots more.

Greater Belfast (on which the following listings focus) is crammed with indoor activities to entertain the family when the weather is poor. One of the city's most appealing attributes is its openness and space, ideal for walking, cycling (see page 121) and golf. There's no excuse not to get active, but if you prefer to watch rather than take part, there is usually a match or sporting event going on somewhere.

Bowling

Hollywood Bowl, Odyssey Pavilion, 2 Queen's Quay; www.hollywoodbowl. co.uk. This twenty-lane bowling alley also has a pool bar, arcade and diner, and is fully licenced.

Xtreme Bowling, Dundonald International Ice Bowl, 111 Old Dundonald Road; www.theicebowl. com. Around twenty minutes from the city centre, this complex also houses Northern Ireland's only public Olympic-size ice rink, and a children's indoor adventure centre.

Golf

Northern Ireland is a golfer's paradise and Belfast has eleven courses within the city boundary, plus scores of others throughout Northern Ireland.

Balmoral Golf Club, 518 Lisburn Road; www.balmoralgolf.com. Literally minutes from the city centre, nearly as venerable as Royal Belfast and more easily accessible. A 2276yd/m parkland course, it was here that champion Irish golfer Fred Daly learnt the ropes. Good clubhouse, too.

Belvoir Park Golf Club, 73 Church Road, Newtownbreda; www.belvoir parkgolfclub.com. Host to Irish opens and judged by South African golf pro Gary Player to be one of the world's best parkland courses. It's also one of the most beautiful.

Castlereagh Hills Golf Course, Upper Braniel Road; www.castlereaghhills. com. This eighteen-hole course has competitive rates and green fees for visitors. A licenced restaurant with an outdoor balcony and views across the hills is a welcoming nineteenth hole.

Royal Belfast Golf Club, Station Road, Craigavad, Holywood; www.royalbelfast.com. The oldest club in Ireland – and one of the best. Not always the easiest to visit (though staying at the adjacent *Culloden Estate and Spa* earns you special access), it has magnificent views of Belfast Lough and a challenging course that attracts leading golfers.

Swimming

Let's Go Hydro, 1 Mealough Road, Carryduff; www.letsgohydro.com. Activities include aqua rugby and

---

Active kids

Kids – especially aspiring farmers – adore Streamvale Open Farm (38 Ballyhanwood Road; www.stream vale.com) with animals to feed, nature trails, play areas, and pony, quad and tractor rides. You can watch the cows being milked every afternoon. Pickie Funpark (Marine Gardens, Bangor; www.pickiefunpark.com; free, prices vary for rides) has been a hit with generations of children. There are giant pedal swans on a lake, a steam train, a mini golf course, playground and colourful Victorian-style beach huts.

---

football, open-water swimming, kayaking, paddle boarding and volleyball. The on-site Puddle Park is for smaller children, and there's a spa and accommodation, too, plus drive-in movie nights.

Walking

Belfast has miles of designated walkways by the river, across hills or through nature reserves and parks. Besides the walking tours available (see page 119), there are various groups

Belvoir Park Golf Club.

and organisations to help you gain the best hiking experience.

Walk NI, www.walkni.com. This useful website lists walks across the region, as well as all the local rambling clubs that organise regular excursions of varying lengths and types in and around Belfast and beyond.

Spectator sports

Athletics

Mary Peters Track, Old Coach Road; www.marypeterstrack.com. Hosts international athletics meetings; its name paying homage to the Northern Irish Olympic gold medallist.

Belfast City Marathon, www.belfast citymarathon.com. Taking place at the beginning of May, the 26-mile (39km) route starts at Stormont and takes in north, south, east and west Belfast. A half-marathon follows in September.

Ball games

Ulster Rugby, Kingspan Stadium, 134 Mount Merrion Avenue; www.ulsterrugby.com. The Ulster rugby union team play both national and international fixtures at their

Hill hiking.

Belfast City Marathon.

Kingspan headquarters, with its family stand and giant LED screens.

National Football Stadium, **Windsor Park**, Donegall Avenue; www.irishfa. com. Home to the Northern Ireland football team. You can book stadium tours and view the artefacts and mixed-media displays in its heritage centre, then get kitted out for match day at the shop.

Casement Park, Andersonstown Road; www.casementpark.ie. Plans are in the pipeline to redevelop Casement Park to make it the place to enjoy Gaelic games.

Horse racing

Down Royal, Maze, Lisburn; www.downroyal.com. Ten miles (16km) south of the city centre, this historic racecourse hosts a series of popular meetings throughout the year.

Ice hockey

Belfast Giants, SSE Arena, 2 Queen's Quay; www.belfastgiants.com. The Giants have built up a huge fan base for this exhilarating sport. The home games, during the season between September and April, are attended by thousands of fans.

Themed holidays

A holiday in Northern Ireland can be more than just the normal sightseeing trip. The region's diversity lends itself to all sorts of interesting ways to spend a vacation.

Creative breaks

Belfast Cookery School, 53–54 Castle Street; www.belfastcookery school.com. Classes for all abilities in Belfast city centre, covering everything from how to cook the perfect steak to making authentic Irish breads and Asian street food.

Loaf Pottery, 24 Main Street, Crawfordsburn; www.loafcatering. com/loafpottery. Profits from sales and classes-with-a-purpose go towards supporting people with disabilities. Try the pizza-and-pottery night or a wheel-throwing workshop.

Health kicks

Strangford Lough Activity Centre, 40 Whiterock Road, Killinchy; www.strangfordloughactivitycentre. com. Canoe-based litter-picking, kayaking with wild food foraging, and full-moon paddles are among the classes. Make memories by greeting a new day with a sunrise paddle-boarding and island-yoga class.

Lake Isle Retreats, Derrylin, Co. Fermanagh; www.lakeisleretreats.com. Spiritual retreats with an emphasis on mindfulness, yoga and vegetarian cooking, based at Mandala House on the shores of idyllic Lough Erne.

Horseriding

Sheans Horse Farm, 38 Cooleeran Road, Armoy, Ballymoney, Co. Antrim; www.sheanshorsefarm.com. Tuition and off-road hacking holidays in the North Antrim hills, an area of outstanding natural beauty.

Walking

A Way a Wee Walk, 20 Ben Eden Green; www.awayaweewalk.com. Daily walking tours of the Giant's Causeway cliff path, as well as holidays around the Causeway Coast and Glens of Antrim.

Themed tours

A History of Terror, www.deadcentre tours.com. Award-winning guides lead the best Troubles tour, explaining the conflict and peace process from a politically neutral position.

Belfast Music Walking Tour, www.creativetoursbelfast.com. Covering classical, trad, rock, punk and more, passionate guide Dolores brims with knowledge about this UNESCO City of Music.

Game of Thrones Tours, www.game ofthronestours.com. Fun for Thronies visiting filming locations from the award-winning series, including the Dark Hedges and Giant's Causeway. Guides were extras on the show.

Paranormal Ghost Tour, www.belfast lad.com. Starting in the seventeenth-century *White's Tavern*, explore the haunted history of old Belfast.

Taste & Tour, www.tasteandtour. co.uk. Popular food and drink tours around Belfast, which take in the likes of historic St George's Market.

A History of Terror tour.

Practical information

Getting there

By air

Belfast International (www.belfas tairport.com), nineteen miles (30km) northwest of the city, is Northern Ireland's busiest airport with connections to the rest of the UK, Europe and the US. Numerous daily services link Belfast International with London Gatwick, Stansted and many other UK airports.

George Best Belfast City Airport (www.belfastcityairport.com), three miles (5km) east of the city centre, has flights to several European cities and UK provincial airports, plus London's City, Heathrow and Gatwick airports.

The Airport Express 300 bus (www. translink.co.uk) runs to the city centre from the Belfast International. George Best Belfast City Airport has rail links to Belfast's Lanyon Place and Great Victoria Street stations and a direct bus link, No. 600, to the city centre. Taxis are plentiful from both airports.

By sea

Stena Line (www.stenaline.co.uk) runs up to six sailings a day each way between Belfast and Cairnryan in Scotland and four daily services on the eight-hour route between Belfast and Liverpool, including overnight crossings. P&O Irish Sea (www.po ferries.com) sails between Cairnryan and Larne, northeast of Belfast.

Getting around

By bus

TransLink (www.translink.co.uk) operates the bus network. The Metro bus serves Belfast and the suburbs; services usually start and end around the City Hall. Fares can be paid on board by card or you can buy Smartlink multi-journey tickets (available in outlets displaying the Smartlink sign, or via the TransLink journey planner app). The Glider bus runs east to west via the Titanic Quarter. Goldline Express and other Ulsterbus services to the rest of Northern Ireland and beyond operate from the Europa or Laganside bus centres.

By train

Northern Ireland Railways, also operated by TransLink, runs services east to Bangor, northeast to Larne, northwest to Derry and south to Dublin. Commuter trains from Central or Great Victoria Street stations to the Botanic station provide easy access to the campus area.

By taxi

There are taxi ranks outside City Hall, the *Crown Liquor Saloon* (AKA *Crown Bar*), airports and main stations. Drivers at Castle Junction pack London-style taxis until full for a particular direction; they also organise tailored tours. Alternatively, call a 'radio cab' such as Value Cabs (tel: 028-9080 9080; www.valuecabs.co.uk) or fonaCAB (tel: 028-9033 3333; www.fonacab. com). Public taxis can be hailed when they have a 'for hire' sign illuminated. Fares are set by the Department of the

Taxi ranks are dotted around the city.

The Metro bus in the city centre.

Environment; private firms have their own rates. If they do not display a meter, ask for the approximate cost in advance, most now take card payments. Uber is also available.

By car

The city has many car parks and lots of on-street pay-and-display parking. Donegall Place and its tributaries are pedestrianised, but only in theory. Drive on the left; speed limits, with clearly signed exceptions, are 30mph (50km/h) in built-up areas, 60mph (95km/h) outside built-up areas and 70mph (112km/h) on motorways.

Most recognised car-hire firms operate from the airports and have city offices. Options include Argus Car Hire (tel: 020-3468 5883; www.arguscarhire.com); Avis (tel: 028-9032 9258; www.avis.co.uk); and Enterprise Rent-a-Car (tel: 0800 111 4312; www.enterprise.co.uk).

By bike

Completion of the National Cycling Network added lots more opportunities for biking in and around the city, with dedicated paths along the River Lagan (see page 71), mandatory cycle lanes in the centre, and out-of-town tracks (free maps from Belfast Welcome Centre). One of the best is the tranquil Comber Greenway which runs eight miles along a disused railway line from east Belfast to Comber. The route, also suitable for walkers, starts at the *Big Fish* sculpture beside the Queen Elizabeth II Bridge, follows the riverside past the SSE Arena, takes in the RMS *Titanic* attractions, the C.S.

Going green

Belfast is becoming increasingly bicycle-friendly and has signed up to Cycle to Work, a UK government initiative to encourage locals to leave their cars at home. It is part of the city's Green Transport Plan and includes helping employees buy bicycles tax free. The Belfast Bikes scheme (www.belfastbikes.co.uk) is a public bike-hire initiative that has the same aim – it now has fifty docking stations and more than four hundred bikes dotted across the city. The city's main cycling routes form part of the UK's National Cycle Network (www.sustrans.org.uk). The Connswater Greenway in east Belfast is a 5.6-mile (9km) route past three rivers, connecting green spaces along a wildlife corridor. Outside the city, the Ulster Way now stretches a staggering 636 miles (1000km) around Northern Ireland, making it the longest circular walking path in the UK and Ireland.

The Ulster Orchestra performing at Waterfront Hall.

Lewis statue and Parliament Buildings at Stormont, along with views of the Belfast hills. To hire a bike, sign up to the public Belfast Bikes scheme (see box; www.belfastbikes.co.uk).

Travel A-Z

Accessible travel

The official tourist information service for Belfast and Northern Ireland (www.visitbelfast.com) has teamed up with AccessAble (www.accessable. co.uk) to assist people with disabilities. It is dedicated to improving access and provides a national accessibility guide online; multiple venues have been researched, including visitor attractions, shops, restaurants, bars, toilets and services.

Most buses, trains and taxis have wheelchair access. Disability Action (www.disabilityaction.org) has useful information, too. The larger taxi firms will have wheelchair-accessible vehicles.

Emergencies

Ambulance, fire, police: dial 999.

For medical and dental emergencies, the main Accident and Emergency hospital is the Royal Victoria (274 Grosvenor Road; www.belfasttrust. hscni.net).

Opening hours

City-centre shops are generally open Mon–Sat 9am–6pm (Thurs until 9pm). Some larger stores open Sun 1–6pm.

Neighbourhood stores and garage forecourt convenience shops often open much longer – 24 hours in some cases.

Tourist information

Major towns throughout Northern Ireland have a tourist information office.

The Visit Belfast Welcome Centre (9 Donegall Square North; www.visit belfast.com) is a one-stop tourist centre with information on accommodation, visitor attractions, tours, events and transport, both for Belfast, the rest of Northern Ireland and the Irish Republic. Multilingual staff can book hotels, concerts and tours. It has a shop, left-luggage facility, bureau de change and internet facilities, as well as drinks machines and free wi-fi. Visit Belfast also has information centres at the city's two airports.

The local tourist office in Derry (1 Waterloo Place; www.visitderry.com) can supply information on the city, book accommodation and give advice on the surrounding area. It also has a great gift shop.

Entertainment

Belfast has earned a good reputation for a new generation of stylish bars and nightclubs, and hotel bars are particularly polished. Traditional pubs (see page 38) remain popular and often provide a venue for live music. There is plenty of opportunity, too, for a night at the theatre or cinema, plus comedy events and concerts.

Nightlife

Belfast was named a UNESCO City of Music in 2021, so it's not difficult to find pubs and other venues with live music. The streets around City Hall and Donegall Square are peppered with trendy bars and clubs. Near Queen's University, *Lavery's* (12–18 Bradbury Place; www.laverysbelfast.com) is one of the city's most iconic fixtures, and a home for generations of youth cultures. It has live music, alternative club nights and a large pool room across four bars and two roof gardens, plus the opportunity to pour your own pint.

Live music in a pub.

The Dirty Onion (3 Hill Street; www.thedirtyonion.com) in the Cathedral Quarter is one of Belfast's new breed of quirkily named bars. It hosts trad and acoustic music sessions and is dog-friendly. Parts of the building are over 300 years old.

In the city centre, *The Tipsy Bird* (90–100 Ann Street; www.thetipsy bird-belfast.co.uk) does a good line in boozy bottomless brunches, drag nights and whimsically named cocktails such as the Sour Bake (bake is Belfast slang for 'face'). Staff still talk about the night in 2021 that pop star Taylor Swift dropped by.

Theatre, cinema and music

The main music, theatre and comedy venues are the Ulster Hall (see page 17), Waterfront Hall (see page 59), Grand Opera House (see page 24), The Belfast Empire (42 Botanic Avenue; www.thebelfastempire.com) and SSE Arena (see page 85). For cinema, the Odeon Belfast (1 Victoria Square; www.odeon.co.uk) has eight screens. Other complexes include the Movie House (City Side Retail Park; www.moviehouse.co.uk); The Avenue (Castle Court Shopping Centre; www. theavenuecinema.com); the Art Deco-era Strand Arts Centre in east Belfast (152–154 Holywood Road; www.

strandartscentre.com) and Cineworld at the SSE Arena (see page 86). Non-mainstream, arthouse and global cinema can be seen at the Queen's Film Theatre (QFT) (see page 50).

LGBTQ+

Centred around the Cathedral Quarter, the LGBTQ+ scene in Belfast is loud, proud and growing. The *Kremlin* (96 Donegall Street; www.kremlin-belfast. com), a Soviet-themed nightclub, is one of the scene's longest-running venues. It's massive, with theme nights. Around the corner is stylish *Union Street* (8–14 Union Street; www.unionstreetbar. com), housed in a converted Victorian shoe factory, hosting drag cabaret, karaoke and movie nights. Beside it, *The Maverick* (1 Union Street; www. themaverickbelfast.com) is another popular Rainbow Quarter hangout.

Belfast Pride (www.belfastpride. com) gets bigger every year, hosting a week of parties, concerts, talks, discos, and a parade around the city centre, usually in late July or early August. The Belfast LGBTQIA+ centre (23–31 Waring Street; www.lgbtni.org) is home to a number of charities and community initiatives, from the health and wellbeing services of the Rainbow Project (www.rainbow-project.org) to a trans resource centre, and hosts events from coffee hour to games nights.

Accommodation

Belfast's growing reputation as a city-break destination means that accommodation prices have risen steeply in recent years. The good news is that the variety and quality has gone up too. From five-star luxury to homely B&Bs, there's an option for all budgets, with, usually, the famed Ulster hospitality evident in the filling breakfasts and general geniality.

Belfast

The 1852

13 Lower Crescent Road;
www.the1852.com.
A boutique hotel occupying a stylishly restored nineteenth-century house in the Queen's Quarter. It's discreetly tucked away, yet on the doorstep of the city's nightlife. It has a chic bar, and its popular *Town Square Café* is perfect for breakfast through to dinner. ££

Botanical Backpackers

63 Fitzwilliam Street;
www.botanicalbackpackers.co.uk.
A welcoming Queen's Quarter hostel a five-minute walk from the university. Based in an old Victorian townhouse, it has a comfy home-from-home vibe with inviting social spaces and friendly staff. £

Bullitt pays homage to the Steve McQueen film.

Bullitt

40a Church Lane;
www.bullitthotel.com.
Named and styled after the uber-cool Steve McQueen film, this is one of Belfast's more hip hotels. Make time to visit rooftop bar and restaurant *Tetto* for a cocktail. The rooms can be on the small side (the smallest size is even named Dinky) but are comfortable and stripped bare of extras to keep prices down. ££

Europa Hotel

Great Victoria Street;
www.europahotelbelfast.com.
Opened in 1971, the *Europa Hotel* is still famous as having once been the world's most bombed hotel, suffering 33 attacks during the Troubles. The decor now is modern and unfussy, and the city-centre location is hard to beat. £££

The Fitzwilliam Hotel

1–3 Great Victoria Street;
www.fitzwilliamhotelbelfast.com.
The interior of this five-star hotel is contemporary, sleek and elegantly designed, with environmentally friendly features and plush bedding. £££

Grand Central

9–15 Bedford Street;
www.grandcentralhotelbelfast.com.
Neutrally decorated rooms come with modern features, but the big attraction is the city-centre location and the

Hotels price guide

Each accommodation reviewed in this Guide is accompanied by a price category, based on the cost of a standard double room in high season, including breakfast.
£ = under £100
££ = £100–£200
£££ = over £200

upper-floor views, especially from the 22nd-floor *Observatory* cocktail bar. £££

The Harrison Chambers of Distinction

45 Malone Road;
www.chambersofdistinction.com.
Opulent chambers decorated with an eclectic selection of artworks, ephemera and antique furniture. Each individually themed bedroom is named after a celebrated figure with a local connection. Accommodation ranges from the bijou Gallivanter room to grand, bay-windowed suites. ££

Malmaison Belfast

34–38 Victoria Street;
www.malmaison.com.
Near the city centre, this imaginative conversion from two beautiful Victorian seed warehouses has dramatic decor plus a popular brasserie and Art Deco bar. ££

The Merchant Hotel

16 Skipper St;
www.themerchanthotel.com.
This opulent five-star hotel in the heart of the Cathedral Quarter is housed in a Grade A-listed Victorian building, a former bank HQ. Rooms are either Art Deco or Victorian in style. £££

The Old Rectory Guesthouse

148 Malone Road;
www.anoldrectory.co.uk.
This delightful Victorian guesthouse in leafy south Belfast is renowned for its award-winning breakfasts. Rooms are charming and individually decorated. ££

Ten Square

10 Donegall Square South;
www.tensquare.co.uk.
A nineteenth-century linen warehouse transformed into a stylish hotel right behind the City Hall. The guest rooms are decorated in a contemporary chic style featuring rain showers and huge plasma televisions. £££

Titanic Hotel Belfast

Queen's Road, Titanic Quarter;
www.titanichotelbelfast.com.

Titanic Hotel Belfast occupies the former HQ of Harland & Wolff.

This sumptuous tribute to Belfast history is the former Victorian HQ of Harland & Wolff, builders of RMS *Titanic*. Authentically restored, architects and artists have maintained the glamour of the listed building, with Art Deco-style bedrooms and wow-factor public spaces. The original domed drawing offices now house a ballroom and a bar/lounge. £££

North

Elephant Rock Hotel

17–19 Lansdowne Crescent, Portrush, County Antrim;
www.elephantrockhotel.co.uk.

The elegant *Grand Room* restaurant in *The Merchant Hotel*.

Finn Lough bubble dome.

This family-run boutique hotel in a Victorian terrace brings a fresh approach to the seaside town. Individually designed rooms offer a glamourous, kitsch vibe; the pick of the bunch have Atlantic views. The restaurant serves fresh local produce. ££

Salthouse Eco-Lodges
Salthouse Hotel, 39 Dunamallaght Road, Ballycastle; www.thesalthousehotel.com. Scattered across the grounds of this sea-facing hotel are several off-grid lodges, powered by renewable wind and solar energy, offering home comforts and stylish decor. Both hotel and lodges have a 'no single-use plastics' policy. £££

West

Killyhevlin Lakeside Hotel & Lodges
Dublin Road, Enniskillen, County Fermanagh; www.killyhevlin.com. With an idyllic waterfront setting, this four-star hotel not only has a clutch of guest rooms but also fourteen self-catering lakeside lodges. Great food, health club, pool and spa. ££

Finn Lough
37 Letter Road, Aghnablaney, Enniskillen; www.finnlough.com. Making full use of its woodland setting on the Fermanagh/Donegal border, Finn Lough has a handful of private, pricey, transparent bubble domes for guests. Forget a sleeping bag on a dusty floor, here, you'll sleep beneath the stars in a four-poster bed. £££

East

The Old Inn
Main Street, Crawfordsburn, County Down; www.theoldinn.com. Established in 1614, this homely-yet-luxurious boutique hideaway bursts with period charm and is home to clutch of individually named rooms. You might even spot singer and local resdent Van Morrison propping up the bar. The Treetop Spa is a newer addition. £££

Portaferry Hotel
10 The Strand, Portaferry, County Down; www.theportni.com. The best of this attractive hotel's rooms overlook Strangford Lough. Staff are fantastically friendly, the bar is cosy, and a slap-up breakfast sets you up for the day. Ask for a four-poster bedroom. ££

Southeast

Slieve Donard
Downs Road, Newcastle, Co. Down; www.marineandlawn.com/slievedonard. With new owners taking the helm in 2021, this landmark resort underwent a long-overdue renovation. Rooms and public areas are now sumptuously furnished, inspired by the landscape, the hotel's Victorian heritage and the area's golfing tradition. Choose a sea room for coastal views. £££